MW00889526

Duct Tape is Not a Behavioral Int

By Laura A. Riffel, Ph.D.

ISBN:

978-1-304-77420-0

©2014 Behavior Doctor Seminars

"We are what we repeatedly do. Excellence, therefore, is not an act but a habit." -

Aristotle

The photo on the front of this book was purchased from 123rf.com by behaviordoctor.org and is not the copyright property of Behavior Doctor Seminars. The photo cannot be reproduced unless purchased from 123rf.com . The photos from Dr. Emoto's experiment were taken from the website and every effort has been made to gain approval for these photos. I do not own the copyright to those pictures. The animated pictures in this book are from www.animationfactory.com and were purchased for use by www.behaviordoctor.org. The other pictures in this book are he property of Behavior Doctor Seminars with one exception taken from Google Images.

Contents

Chapter One: Classroom Set-up Strategies 11

    Theme 13

    Passes 15

    Interruptions 15

    Room Arrangement 16

    Desk Arrangement 17

    Desk Preparation 17

    Chairs 18

    Lights 19

    Bulletin Boards 20

    Feng Shui: Explanation of each area: 21

    Turn-in Procedures 25

    Mailboxes (elementary) 25

    Rubrics 27

    Organization 29

    Expectations 31

    Teach the Behavior through Video Modeling 32

    Website 36

Chapter Two: Ambiance 38

    Effects of Words on Water 39

    Effects of Words on Rice 39

    Misteaks are Learning Opportunities 40

    Positive Message of the Day 41

    Comfort 43

    Shoes 43

    Mindfulness 44

    Music and Subliminal Messages 46

Chapter Three: The First Week of School 48

    On the First Day of School 48

    Circle Time (for elementary) 49

        Personal Space 49

Koosh Ball 50

Expectations 50

Voice Level 52

Areas of the room 53

Desks 54

Pledge 55

Positive Notes 56

Love Notes 56

Secondary Students and Love Notes 58

Positive Notes 59

Final Thoughts on Positive Notes 59

That's Not Fair 60

Class Meetings 63

Chapter Four: Academic Strategies to Begin the Year 64

Traits of Awesome Teachers 64

First Writing Assignment 66

Three Stars and a Wish 67

Pencils 69

Test Taking Strategies 70

To reduce stress: 70

To combat hopelessness 70

To Reduce Anxiety 71

Combating lack of Ownership (why do I care?) 71

To Attack Distractions During the Test 72

Exit Slips 72

Name Tag Learning 74

Gatekeeper 74

Grading Papers 75

Schedule Colors 76

Chapter Five: Contingencies and Rewards 77

Preparation 77

Group Contingencies: Group Rewards 77

Group vs. Group Contingency..87

Cafeteria..89

Tardies to class..89

Prizes for "BEST" behavior in any special class (Elementary)..89

More ideas for the whole school..90

Individual Contingencies: Group Rewards..93

   Secret Agent..93

   Secret Line Walker: (Elementary)..94

Chapter Six: Secondary or Targeted Group Interventions:..95

Pot Holder Loops..95

Student-Teacher Rating Sheet..95

Student Copy of Teacher Student Rating Sheet..98

Chapter Seven: Specific Behaviors and Interventions..100

Assess Learning Capabilities..102

Assess Physical Well-Being..103

Assess Sensory Overload..104

Check-in/Check-out (CICO)..106

Class Helper or Class Job..109

Class Teacher..112

Counseling..113

Diversionary..114

Equal Choices..115

Equal Choices in Right Ear..116

Fidget Tools..117

First/Then (Now/Then)..118

Hula-Hoop..120

Good Try..120

Organizational Self-Help Skills..121

Power Card..123

Private Meeting..124

Secret Signal..125

Sensory Diet..126

Social Skills Training 127

Stop, Walk, & Talk 129

Three B's (Be quick, Be quiet, Be gone) 130

Three Stars and a Wish 130

Token Economy 131

TUMS 131

Vanna White 132

Video Self-Modeling 133

Chapter Eight: Odds and Ends 135

For Student's Prior Cognitive Ability 138

Instructional Quality and Quantity 140

Direct Instruction 141

Acceleration in Learning 142

Multiple Intelligences based on Howard Gardner's Work.................................... 143

Home Factors 144

Remediation Feedback 145

Measuring Progress 145

Restructuring the Day 146

Zero Students Failing Zero Classes.. 147

Whatever it Takes: How Professional Learning Communities Respond When Kids Don't Learn 147

Worksheets You Can Use 148

Shopping List... 151

Funk Sway for Your Classroom 152

Desk Planning.. 153

List of Positive Words for Your Classroom 154

Rewards Teachers Can Give to Students: 157

Free or Inexpensive Rewards for Parents 162

Young Children 162

Teenagers.. 166

Tweets... 168

References 171

Movie Clips Used in the Presentation.. 173

Duct Tape is Not a Behavioral Intervention

Why such a wacky title?

An Indiana couple is looking for answers from their daughter's former elementary school after the 8-year-old came home from her special-needs program with her shoes duct-taped to her feet and ankles (February 2013).

KIRKLAND, Wash. -- The Lake Washington School District has placed a teacher on leave for allegedly taping a student to a chair (May 2013).

FRESNO, Calif. (KFSN) -- Action News has learned a Valley teacher is under investigation after students say he had them duct tape their mouths in his class. The Madera Unified superintendent confirmed Tuesday afternoon an elementary school teacher is under investigation (September 2013).

OCEAN SPRINGS, Mississippi -- A 6th grade teacher at Ocean Springs Upper Elementary was disciplined for duct-taping a male student's mouth shut when he was too talkative in class (October 2013).

A Buchtel student has filed a lawsuit against his former math teacher who was fired in May for uploading photographs of students with duct-taped mouths (October 2013).

The list goes on, these are just a few of the top headlines. Are the adults who carried out these deeds terrible people? I do not think they meant to be terrible, I think anyone who does not have enough tools in their tool belt can make horrific mistakes. It is our job in pre-service, professional development, and trainings to provide educators and adults who work with children more tools for their tool belt. This book focuses on providing tools from the beginning to the end.

Dealing with behavior in the classroom is one of the most frequent requests for service. This book will focus on proactive strategies you can use in your classroom to assist in the amelioration of behavioral issues. A few of these are review from previous presentations; however, the majority of the material is new and focuses on what you can do to set your room up for success.

We will begin with setting up your classroom on the first day and preparation tactics to set up your classroom for success. Rather than wait for behavior to show up in the classroom and react to the behavior, we will share ideas on proactive strategies before the behavior has a chance to show up. The ideas of this book are based on over 30 years of teaching Pre-K through adults in regular and special education.

My daughter is changing careers and beginning her new career as a teacher. I dedicate this book to her as she joins this fine profession. I am so proud of the woman she has become and seeing her love for helping children learn to shine inspires me all over again.

Although this book is geared for the beginning of the year, it will have a lot of ideas that can be useful for any returning teacher. The beginning of the book will focus on setting up the room prior to the students' arrival. The middle of the book will focus on things to do the first weeks of school and the final section of the book will focus on what to do when a student has a behavior you would like to target for change.

Here are some real uses for duct tape in the classroom:

- Black and white duct tape stripes on the front of the coaches' desk- mimics the referee stripe.
- Covering mailboxes for students to turn-in work or to pick up notes home.
- Covering old ice cream containers from Baskin Robbins to make book bins for reading corner.
- Great for holding up the hems of dresses that come undone- also works for pant hems.
- Great for putting on the edges of rough or broken furniture or cabinetry that typically snags your clothing as you walk by.
- Prom dresses and tuxedos have been made from duct tape.
- Reflective duct tape is useful in Iceland to find student's jackets in the snow on a dark day.
- Stagecraft and Drama teachers can think of tons of uses for play props- even costumes.
- To cover the ends of a pool noodle which has been cut into fifths. Run pantyhose through the middle of the pool noodle and tie the pantyhose to either side of the chair legs. The duct tape keeps the pantyhose from cutting through the pool noodle. This makes a great foot fidget for students who need to move.
- To designate a giant square on the floor for where the calendar time will occur in an elementary classroom.
- To make a design on a lunch bag that looks like everyone else's.
- To mark spots to stand on the floor when lining up.
- To patch up a backpack that doesn't quite make it to the end of the year.
- To patch up torn jeans when playing on the playground.
- To put on the bottom of slick shoes to keep children from slipping on tile floors or on slick stage.
- Use it as a book cover for a book that might get wet (such as in art class, cooking class, or shop class).
- Use it to build up one side of a wobbly chair when the tip gets lost.
- Use it to hold together a notebook that has almost broken through. This will keep it together till the end of the year.

Chapter One: Classroom Set-up Strategies

I remember my first day of reporting for contract as a teacher with my own classroom. I did not know where to start. I started by making my desk look neat and organized and then I was stumped: 1) room arrangement with good flow, 2) lighting, 3) circle area, or a 4) science area. I didn't know where I should start or how to go about setting it up. This booklet is to help first year teachers who did their student teaching and already came into a room set up for them and want some help getting their room ready. This is also a book for veteran teachers with classroom management strategies for those behaviors that you would like to target for change.

I now have over thirty years in education under my belt and I've learned a few things. I learn new things every year. My first year of teaching, I moved things around every other week. Now I know that upsets those children who have difficulty with transitions. It's not that your room needs to stay the same all year, but the changes should be minimized and announced to the students. The changes should occur during natural breaks, or if the students are older the students themselves can help with the moving of desks. Be careful not to ask students to move something that is top-heavy or could break or fall on them.

We will begin this book with what to do before the students ever arrive.

Prior to the first day of school

Scope out the following in your new building: 1) restrooms, 2) water fountain, 3) library, 4) exit doors, and 5) special classes they may attend if you are primary. If you are secondary, scope out where your students' lockers will be. Students have reported having to carry 50 pounds of books because they don't have time to go to their lockers in between classes. If this is true for you, offer to keep the books in the classroom. Request an extra set of books for the classroom and let students keep their books at home. This alleviates a lot of problems on forgetting books for homework assignments or studying and not having books in the classroom.

Many times, teachers will say to me, "But that's not teaching them responsibility." I think a lot of times educators use this as an excuse because they do not want to deal with something. As a presenter who presents to adults, I cannot tell you how many times adults come to seminars without writing utensils, handouts sent ahead of time, required computers for data collection, not doing their assignments prior to class and so on. I'm quite sure these participants had teachers who "held them accountable" to teach them responsibility and yet they still forget important items. I will give you tips later on to teach responsibility to students, for now, let's agree that carrying 50 pounds of books as a growing teenager is not good for their posture.

Theme

It's always fun to have a theme each year. Your theme should be cute, but not too stimulating. Every summer I always painted a mural on one wall to match my theme. One year, I was teaching third grade and I painted a rainforest theme on my wall. The wall was so busy and bright. I made curtains with rainforest frogs and had all kinds of parrots as my special theme product. The energy in the room was very high that year. The next year, I looped with the same students into fourth grade. I painted a nice peaceful soft blues and greens ocean theme on my wall. The students were much calmer. It's okay to have a zebra theme or leopard theme, just don't paint the whole wall to match, as that is too much. Eric Jensen, who studies brain research, indicates light blue is a calming color and should be used as an accent wall. The other three walls should be a warm light yellow (Jensen, 2005).

This is true for secondary teachers as well. I've been in way too many junior high, middle school, and high school classrooms that had no personality. Not decorating your room sends a message to your students that you do not care about what you are doing. Put up paper or material on the bulletin boards. Put up borders and make the bulletin boards engaging.

You'll want to have a special chair for the student of the day. It's very easy to recover an old office chair with wheels and this can match your classroom theme. At the secondary level, you will want to number all your chairs. Make ice cream sticks with the same numbers on them. When the bell rings, draw a number. Whatever number you draw, that student gets to sit in the special chair. If they are tardy to class, they are exempt from earning the chair. This encourages students to be in their chairs when the bell rings.

You might also have a rocker with a pillow that matches your theme. Putting a rocker in your room will help those students who need proprioceptive input. Get a simple lap desk and let students earn time in the rocker. The more proprioceptive input they need, the more you can help them "win" time in the rocker.

You can recover desk blotters and cup holders with your theme so that everything on your desk matches. Personalize your desk with some pictures of your real life. It's important for students to relate to you as a person. Put up pictures of your pets, children, or leisure activities so the students can relate to you.

Passes

Think about where you will want to hang your passes for students who need to use the restroom, get a drink, return a book to the library, or be excused to "cool down" with the counselor. The passes should be near the door for easy retrieval and return. The self-sticking hooks that peel easily off without ruining the wall work well to hang your passes. Passes can be the cute plastic ones you purchase at a teacher supply store or a simple 3 x 5 card laminated in 10ml laminating film with a hole punched in it. One year I had a cute resin parrot that sat on my desk (left over from a previous year's theme). The students would come up and get it and set it on their desk if they needed to go to the restroom. If I was busy with a reading group, I did not want to have a ton of interruptions with students requesting bathroom passes. This alleviated the interruptions and if anyone "over-used" the privilege, we had private discussions.

Interruptions

Think about how you will handle interruptions. If you think about it before, it will not be a problem during class time. If you are a primary teacher (Pre-K through Sixth) and you teach reading in groups, you will want to have a cue that it is not okay to interrupt the group with questions. Here are some of the best strategies other teachers have used:

- Ask three before me: The students are instructed to ask three other people what they should do before they ask the teacher if the teacher is occupied with someone else (poster in the back of this book). This would be for questions like:

    o Where do I turn this in?

    o How did she say to do this?

    o How much time do we have left?

    o When is this due?

- Some teachers use a punch light from the $1 store with the words "NO Questions" on it in a permanent marker. When the teacher starts his or her group, he/she turns the light on and if someone comes up to interrupt, he/she points to the light.

- Making a sign that says "Ask 3 before me" and placing it near your group work table so you can point to it when someone lingers nearby, can be really helpful. See mini poster in the tools section of this book.

Room Arrangement

Businesses spend millions of dollars hiring designers to tell them what will make a productive work place. More businesses spend thousands of dollars on Feng Shui for the work place to make it a productive work place. The things they consider are: furniture arrangement, color, organization, and ambiance. The

National Education Association (NEA) recommends feng shui for the classroom.

Desk Arrangement

- Put student desks in a curved "U" shape

    o This allows each student to be "front row"

    o The students will be within arm's reach

- Put podium or small teacher table in the middle of the "U" shape (note-this is not the teacher's desk)

- Make sure desks are facing white board, Smartboard™, or chalkboard

- Sit in every chair and see if you can see the board and the small teacher table from a student angle

Desk Preparation

- Put strip of Velcro under the desktop on right hand or left hand edge, or

- Put bathtub applique under the desktop on right hand or left hand edge

The reason for putting this under the desk to help students fidget appropriately. Adults have figured out how to be socially appropriate with their fidgeting for the most part (not counting the people who are umbillically attached to their cell phones). We need to teach students how to be socially appropriate. Fidgeting increases retention by 39% (National Institute of Health, 2013).

Chairs

- Find cushions for the chairs

  - Air-filled Yoga-Pilates air filled disks

  - Kitchen cushions

  - Foam cushions (stadium cushions, garden kneeling pad)

    - Go to a business like a bank and see if they have any promotional items that were stadium cushions you could use

  - Camping pillows

  - Foam disks from IKEA in the children's department (only available at the store)

- Banding between chair legs

  - Physical therapy bands

  - Pantyhose leg

  - Run band or pantyhose through center of cut down pool noodle on each chair

Adults twirl their feet back and forth, bounce their leg, flip their shoe loose and so on during sit and get trainings. We need to teach students how to give themselves proprioceptive input through foot fidgeting in socially appropriate ways. By putting bands on the chairs and teaching students to bounce their foot on it, push it down, pull it up, push from behind it, or take 1/5 of a pool noodle and run the band through and teach the child to slip their shoes off and rub their feet back and forth on the pool noodle. Taking off your shoes and wiggling your toes reduces anxiety by 39% (University of Michigan, 2011).

Lights

The normally unnoticeable 100–120 Hz flicker from fluorescent tubes powered by electromagnetic ballasts are associated with headaches and eyestrain. Individuals with high flicker fusion threshold are particularly affected by electromagnetic ballasts: their EEG alpha waves are markedly attenuated and they perform office tasks with greater speed and decreased accuracy. Ordinary people have better reading performance using high frequency (20 kHz – 60 kHz) electronic ballasts than electromagnetic ballasts (Küller & Laike, 1998).

- Fluorescent lights- check out www.huelight.net – write a grant at www.donorschoose.org and request panels for your classroom
- If you cannot get the special panels which decrease the flickering and glare from the fluorescent lights, try having the custodian remove every other bulb so it decreases the glare and flicker in the room

Bulletin Boards

- Using the components of Feng Shui in the classroom your room should have

  the following colors in the following places: (See the diagram). Businesses

  spend big money having designers come in and implement the practices of Feng

  Shui in their place of business to increase productivity, increase sales, and

  create harmony in the workplace. While you may not think you are selling

  anything, in reality you are selling the idea of becoming a life-long learner.

  Anything we do to make the environment conducive to life-long learning and

  loving learning is a step in the right direction.

Purple bulletin board	Red bulletin board	Pink bulletin board
<ul><li>Clinic or Spa area</li><li>Posters of nature</li><li>60 bpm music</li><li>Relaxation posters</li><li>Water feature</li><li>Blue bean bag</li></ul>	<ul><li>Battery operated candle</li><li>Gotcha tallies</li><li>Social information</li></ul>	<ul><li>Team points</li><li>Team divisions if using whole brain teaching</li></ul>
Green bulletin board	Yellow rug	White bulletin board
<ul><li>Round wooden table</li><li>Student pictures</li></ul>		<ul><li>White round table</li><li>White metal clock</li><li>Extended learning</li></ul>
Blue bulletin board	Doorway should be navy	Gray bulletin board
<ul><li>Pictures of heroes</li></ul> Based on the work of Heiss (2004)	<ul><li>Pictures of class</li><li>Pictures of you outside school</li></ul>	<ul><li>Silver box</li><li>Wind chime</li><li>Globe</li></ul>

Feng Shui: Explanation of each area:

- Purple (This is your "hokey pokey" clinic "Where you turn yourself around.")

  - Clinic or Spa area- Don't think of this as a "time-out" corner – but a place to get your thoughts together. Students will use it on their own without disrupting the class if you set it up this way.

  - Posters of nature- Pictures of nature are anxiety reducing and most students who are upset are anxious about something.

  - 60 bpm music- The resting heart rate is 60 bpm and yet we find students who are aggressive tend to have heart rates that range in the average of 147 bpm. Music therapy suggests our hearts will match the music we are listening to. Play 60 bpm in this area or have a headphone and music available for students to listen to while getting themselves turned around.

  - Relaxation posters- Have posters about breathing back in this area. For example a simple breathing technique like putting your tongue behind your two front teeth, closing your mouth and breathing in for a four count and out for a four count through your nose. If repeated 10 times it will slow your breathing down.

Another technique for reducing an obsessive thought is to put your five fingers on your forehead and lifting each one up and back down two times. As you do this look up toward each finger. This action will help erase the obsessive thought.

- o Water feature- Running water is calming. A small fountain plugged in near this area will help students relax and get their thoughts together so they can come back to the area cool, calm and collected.

- o Blue bean bag- Your blue bean bag should be made of pleather for several reasons: 1) it's a cool material and 2) it's less likely to absorb critters of the lice variety. When students are upset they tend to get hot, sitting into the cool bean bag will help cool them down, it's a nice sensory hug without touching someone.

- Red Bulletin Board

  - o Battery operated candle- Candles make places seem homey. Since the fire marshal frowns on real candles, a battery operated one will work.

  - o Gotcha tallies- This is important information. In your school, the teachers will be giving out "gotchas" if you are a (school-wide positive behavioral interventions and supports (PBIS) school and it is nice to keep a tally of how many tallies have been received by the room or the hour. Do not post individual names with tallies aside them because this would cause hurt feelings. Keep those tallies private and let other teachers know when a student has not received a tally for a while so they can catch them being good. If you are not a PBIS school, this can be where you keep your compliment board. We will discuss compliment board in the group contingency-group reward area below.

- Social information- This is where you should post information about upcoming events that might be of interest to parents and students, the lunch calendar, and school vacation information etc.

• Pink bulletin board- This does not have to be a bulletin board. It can be a piece of pink tag board that is laminated. This area is for your group vs. group contingency. We will describe that in the contingency reward section below under group vs. group contingency.

- Team points- You might have your class divided into the North vs. the South if you are a history teacher, or the peanut butters and the jellies if you are a kindergarten teacher. You might also have four groups instead of two based on how the students are grouped in cooperative grouping situations.

- o Team divisions if using whole brain teaching- Label the teams in this area and who is on what team. If you are a secondary teacher, you can even have the teams be Hour One, Hour Two, and Hour Three and so on.

- Green bulletin board- This does not have to be a bulletin board either- you can use a green piece of tag board which is laminated. Ask students to bring in pictures of themselves to put up in the room. This gives it a homey feel and makes the students feel like they are part of a family.

  - o Round wooden table- This round table will be where you meet with students to discuss work or help with individual needs.

  - o Student pictures- Send out a post card asking students to bring a picture of themselves when they come to "Sneak a Peak" night to put up on the bulletin board. This is a nice way to introduce yourself to them and as you put their picture up that night, you will get to meet them and their parents.

- In the center of the room, you will put a yellow rug. This will be where you will stand so your podium or presentation table will be on this yellow rug.

Turn-in Procedures

Bins in the following colors:

- Red-reading

- Orange-language

- Yellow-math

- Green-Social Studies

- Blue-Science

- Purple-Other

Place the bins on a shelf near the door

Label the bins for each subject

Mailboxes (elementary)

These are usually purchased through office supply; however, you might get lucky and find one at a garage sale. One year I used empty ice cream tubs from Baskin Robbins Ice Cream. You need to have approximately 30 cubby spaces and be large enough for 8.5 by 11 sheets of paper so the students can put their graded work in the bins to take home at the end of the day. This makes it easier for you to pass out notes to parents, copies of your lesson plans, and weekly reader order forms etc. These are some of the items other teachers have used as mailboxes:

- Transparent hanging shoe bags for 15 pairs of shoes
- Former paper organizers from office supplies
- Commercially purchased boxes and then covered with contact paper to match classroom theme
- Same size cereal boxes stacked after covering inside and out with contact paper
- Rolling drawer carts from an office supply store- you may need two or three of them though and this will take up precious space
- An old cabinet with shelves put in about 4 inches apart so there are enough shelves for each student to have one
- Shoe organizer shelves

For labeling boxes, you can put the student's names on the end of brightly colored binder clips and attach them to the box so that the name looks out. This way if a new student moves in and you want to put them in alphabetical order, you can move everyone around easily. If you are labeling the see through shoe pockets, you can make a laminated card decorated in your classroom theme with each student's name on the front. Put this in the clear pocket and you will be able to see the names and easily change it if a new student moves in. You can also take the first day of school picture and laminate a copy on the name card and place that in the pocket. When the last day of school comes around, you can take another picture of the student and put that on another card labeled last day of school. Parents will really appreciate this.

Rubrics

- Make a rubric poster of what good work looks like for each subject. There are some really great samples on Pinterest for each subject and many different grade levels. Type in "rubric" in the search. Here an example- you will adjust based on the age level you work with in your classroom and for every subject:

Written Language

Best	While some people might prefer a relationship with people, I prefer my friendships with my lumbering 201 pound English Mastiff, my persnickety aging calico cat, and my brilliant saltwater Clownfish. Brutus, my English Mastiff still thinks he is a puppy and tries to sit on my lap when I sit down at my computer. Many times when I take him for a walk, people who are coming toward us are quite afraid of him because of his size being double that of the person walking him. Cleopatra, my aging calico cat has a mind of her own and is not easily swayed in her pursuits toward remaining solitary. She does manage to show up whenever she hears a can-opener and can move at lightning speed if the can happens to be of the tuna fish variety. Although it is an expensive hobby, I enjoy a saltwater tank filled with colorful reef fish including my favorite, the Clownfish. My Clownfish are brilliant because they will follow my finger as I trace it back and forth across the side of the tank when it is time to feed them. People can let you down, but my faithful sidekick Brutus, my finicky old cat Cleopatra and my gifted Clownfish never let me down because they entertain me and make me smile.
Better	This man's best friend is a big dog, a finicky cat, and a striped fish. My dog is an English Mastiff and he weighs 201 pounds. People are scared of Brutus when they see him coming. My finicky cat is a calico fur ball I call Cleopatra. Cleopatra is what you would call aloof. I have a huge saltwater tank filled with reef fish. My favorite fish are the clown fish because they follow my finger when I put it up to the tank. I'm quite entertained by my three favorite pets, a dog, a cat, and a striped Clown fish.

Good	I have three pets: a dog, a cat and a fish. My dog is an English Mastiff. My dog's name is Brutus. I have a calico cat that I call Cleopatra. Cleopatra is very aloof and doesn't like to be around people. I have an aquarium of fish, but my favorite fish is a clownfish. My clownfish will follow my finger when I put it up to the tank. I am quite entertained by my three pets.
Poor	I have a cat. The cat's name is Inky. My cat meow's when it is hungry. Dogs are better than cats because they wag their tails. Dogs can be black, brown, white or tiger striped, or spotted.

Organization

Folders. Purchase or order the following colors of folders for each student in your class if you are elementary – or as a school at the secondary level, determine the color code you will use and everyone in the school is consistent

- o Red= Reading type classes (Literature, etc.)

- o Orange= Language type classes (Composition, etc.)

- o Yellow= Math type classes (Algebra, Geometry, etc.)

- o Green= Social Studies type classes (Civics, History etc.)

- o Blue= Science type classes (Biology, etc.)

- o Purple= Specials (electives etc.)

- o For all the folders, do the following:

- Put a sticker on the left pocket labeled "HOMEWORK" and a sticker on the right pocket labeled "Completed Work"

- When you give students Xerox® copies for each subject, run a marker down the side of the stack so that there is a tinge of the correct color on the edge of the paper. This will cue the student as to what folder to put it in. If the student creates the paper by using their own notebook paper, cue them verbally to put a specific color dot in the upper right hand corner of the paper. This will also cue the student in to which bin to turn their work in when they do so.

Bins. Make sure your turn in bins match the color of the subject the students are turning in for their work. For instance, use a red bin for reading assignments. It will save you time if the students are cued visually.

Luggage tags. For students, ask parents to send in a luggage tag. These can be purchased at stores that sell everything for $1. Flip the address label over and write on the back of the tag everything that should go inside the backpack. Give each student a non-permanent marker and teach them to check off each item as it goes into the backpack. This prevents them from forgetting important items. You might have different color cards for each day of the week. For instance, if Library class is on Wednesday, the Tuesday night card would say, "Bring your library book to school tomorrow."

Expectations

- If your school has School-wide Positive Behavioral Interventions and Supports, make sure you have the expectations posted in your classroom with examples of what those expectations should look like, sound like and feel like. I always think of this when teaching behaviors:

  - Head: What do you want the students to think?

  - Heart: What do you want the students to feel?

  - Hands: What do you physically want the students to do?

If your school does not have School-wide PBIS, develop your own 3-5 positively stated expectations. Here are some examples:

- Be Respectful

- Be Responsible

- Be Safe

- Respect Yourself

- Respect Others

- Respect Property

- Make wise choices

- Practice Politeness

- Work Hard

- Show Respect

Teach the Behavior through Video Modeling

- When school starts you will make a video using your students giving examples of what each of your three to five behaviors looks like, sounds like, and feels like: (Here are some samples)

  - In the classroom

    - Raise hand and wait to be called on

    - Raise hand and ask permission to use the restroom

    - Start work soon after assigned

    - Say "Please" and "Thank you"

    - Use kind words

    - Do your best work

  - In the hallway

    - Hands at side

    - Walk on the right in the third row of squares

    - Bubble in mouth

- Eyes watching person in front

- In the cafeteria

  - Have your meal card or number ready

  - Buy only the food you will eat

  - Eat only your food

  - Use your napkin

  - Say "Please" and "Thank you" to the cafeteria staff

  - Use your 6 inch voice and only talk to person on your right, left, or straight in front of you

  - Raise your hand to ask permission to throw your tray away

  - Clean up your area

- On the stairs

  - Walk on the right

  - Use the handrail

  - One step at a time

  - Keep a safe distance from person in front

- In the bathroom

- On the playground

  - What does it look like for four square?

- What does it look like for basketball?

- What does it look like for the slides?

- What does it look like for the tether ball?

- What does it look like for the swings?

- What does it look like on the soccer field?

- What does it look like for hopscotch?

- What does it look like for jump rope?

o In the parking lot

  - Elementary- unloading and loading of cars

  - Middle school- unloading and loading of cars

  - High school

    • Parking courtesy

    • Speed limit

    • What to do if you have a fender bender

    • Lock your car

    • Watch for pedestrians

o On the bus

  - Say "Please" and "Thank you" to the driver

  - Feet on the ground

- Sit facing forward

- Use a six inch voice

- Keep food in backpack

- Pick up trash

- Watch for your stop

- Use the handrail

- Use one step at a time

- Don't cross till you get the signal from the driver

o On the front sidewalks

- Walk on the right

- Stay a hula-hoop distance from the person in front of you

- Stay on the sidewalk

o In the commons area

- Use your zero inch voice during school

- Use your six inch voice before and after school

- Walk on the right

- Pick up trash

- Report any spills on the floor

Website

Set up a class website. There are many free WYSIWYG websites out there. WYSIWYG is "what you see is what you get". You do not have to know coding or have special Internet technology skills. Video tape or audio record your lessons so students can re-listen to them at home and share their learning with their parents. If you believe in homework (and you should read the research first)-then consider video-taping your lessons in private and posting them and then have the students actually do the work in the classroom. This way you can cover for misrules they picked up from the lesson and ensure each student is doing their own work. These are the other things you should consider putting on your website:

- Whole class positive behavior specific praise, "I'm so proud of the way the class handled the fire drill today."

- Upcoming events at the school

- Pictures of your rubrics you created for each subject

- Videos of what good behavior looks like, sounds like, and feels like (get permission first to post because there are students on the video). The students won't be individually labeled by name- but it's best to check with parents first before you put the pictures online.

- Your lesson plans

- If a student is absent, the parents can access the work done that day

- Parents will read what you are teaching and send in artifacts that might help

  - For instance, I was teaching open and closed circuits in fourth grade Science. A dad sent in a doll that formed a circuit when you touched both hands and she laughed- if only one hand was held, the circuit was not connected so it didn't laugh. He also sent in various types of Christmas lights that represented open and closed circuits. I had parents send in dolls, coins, stamps, food, etc. from foreign countries when we studied them.

Ambiance is the tone you feel when you walk into a room. There really is no excuse for a barren or cold feeling room now that Pinterest is filled with excellent ideas. If you are not artistic, trade skills with another teacher. You grade some papers for them and they decorate your room.

Ambiance isn't just how the room looks though. Ambiance is the silent messages your room sends out to your students. Signs like this are bad ambiance:

- Your Mama Doesn't Work Here, so Clean up After Yourself

- No Gossip- No Whining- No Disrespect (tell kids what to do- not what not to do)

- No Slackers Allowed

- Whiners will be Voted off the Island

In the back of this book are two pages of positive words you can use in your classroom. These can be part of bulletin boards, things you write on student papers, and messages you put on your agenda board. The power of intention shows that what you put into something is what you get out of it.

Effects of Words on Water

Dr. Emoto did experiments on water. He had people look at water in containers and read positive and negative words associated with each container of water. He crystalized the water all the same way and the water that had had positive thoughts was beautiful and the water that had had negative thoughts was a jumbled mess. The video of the water crystals is listed in the back of this book.

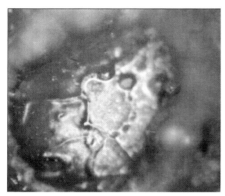 

Same water from Fujiwara Dam- before prayer and after prayer.

Effects of Words on Rice

Dr. Jenna Pollard Sage took two containers of rice. One container of rice had the words "I hate you" and the other container of rice had the words "I love you". Each day she spent time sending the corresponding thoughts to the rice. After one week, the rice that was hated was already forming mold and hair like substance, while the loved rice was still looking edible.

This might be a great experiment to suggest to your students to illustrate the power of thoughts and words. Be sure to put as many positive words around the room as possible.

Misteaks are Learning Opportunities

Every year, I painted the words "Misteaks are Learning Opportunities" on my wall. I waited for the students to notice that the word mistakes was misspelled. I would then model how to look up a word in the dictionary and then I would get out a can of red paint and a step ladder and paint over the misspelled word. As the year progressed, if the students messed up in any way (behavior or academic), I would say, "That's okay. Mistakes are learning opportunities. What did you learn?" I wanted the students to understand that a mistake is not the end of the world and to be more tolerant of themselves and of others. I made sure to point out my own mistakes when I made them and sometimes I made them on purpose, just to emphasize the point.

Positive Message of the Day

I suggest purchasing a plastic picture frame from the dollar store and replacing the stock picture with some solid construction paper in a happy bright color. Each day draw a name and hand a list of positive quotes to that student. The next morning or next class, it is that student's job to get into the classroom and write the positive message of the day. The student will then read the message to the class. This might sound like fluff that you do not have time for; however, if you decrease the stress, anxiety, and negative feelings in the classroom, you will have less disruptions. Less disruptions means more time for teaching. We will talk more about positive messages directly to students in Chapter three.

You Receive What You Project

When I taught, I told the students that the principal liked me better than anyone else and that was why he always gave me the best classes. The students rose a little taller when I told them that. Of course, to my previous colleagues (I am lying here- he/she didn't like me better). I got better students because I believed and my students believed I had better students. It doesn't hurt to tell a little positive intention lie to get what you want. Throughout the year I would say things like:

- "Wow, I always have the smartest students."

- "I always get the students with the best behavior."

- "I am the luckiest teacher alive."

Because it was not said with sarcasm, or said like I didn't believe it, I never had it backfire on me. I have shared this with a few teachers who told me it didn't work for them. I truly believe it didn't work because they didn't believe.

Remember when you were a kid and you clapped because you believed in fairies when Tinkerbelle drank the poison and was dying? (Maybe I'm showing my age here). We have to believe we have the cream of the crop and that is what we will get. You will see this in print more than once: "Energy flows where attention goes." The energy in the room will flow toward positive if that is where the attention of the room is focused. Make sure every word up in your classroom and written on paper for the students to see exudes your belief in them. Even if they blow a test, focus on the ones they got correct.

Comfort

You spend from 8-10 hours a day in this room. It is your home away from home. You should be comfortable if you want to exude comfort to your students. Make sure your room is warm and inviting to you. Do you have a comfortable chair to sit on when the students are not there? Do you have a way to unwind when the students are not there? (music, chocolate, yoga mat, etc.) Even five minutes of yoga or a small piece of dark chocolate, or listening to your favorite music can rejuvenate you during lunch. Do not push yourself so hard that you do not take care of yourself. Your nervous energy will be an ambiance the students can pick up on in the classroom.

Shoes

If your feet hurt, it is difficult to think straight. If you teach elementary, encourage parents to send in slippers for their children to wear during the time in the classroom. Three reasons for this (1) kids can wiggle their toes in slippers which reduces anxiety, (2) softer soles are quieter when the students are walking around, and (3) relaxed students tend to be calmer students. The other reason for having students wear slippers is that you can then wear slippers and look appropriate. Of course the students will have to wear regular shoes outdoors and to PE. However, in the event of a fire drill, the slippers are just fine.

At the secondary level, tell the students they have earned a slipper day in the classroom and they can bring slippers to wear in class the next day. The more they have good manners, the more they can bring their slippers. Look for every opportunity to let them earn the slippers. The students will be calmer.

One teacher on Pinterest had her students bring slippers and wear them during tests. I would call them my Star Student Slippers and have students wear them during any tests. One of the top prize reinforcers for secondary students in my year-long survey was wearing slippers to school, so this is not just for the little kids.

Mindfulness
I'm putting this under ambiance because I feel that mindfulness is part of the "feeling" of the classroom. Mindfulness is a strategy developed by Jean-Gabrielle Larochette. He developed this technique to help his students be present in class.

Larochette said, "The only way we can academically reach children and help them excel in school, is to teach them how to have the stillness it takes to pay attention, stay on task, regulate themselves and make good choices." As we will state throughout this book, we cannot just tell students to "be good". We have to teach students what it means to calm down, to be still, and to really take in the information.

Research of mindfulness programs have found that even a few minutes a day of regular practice improves student self-control and helps increase their participation in class, higher respect rates, feelings of happiness and optimism, and higher levels of self-acceptance. When students practice mindfulness it reduces activity in the amygdala; which, is the emotional center of the brain, responsible for fear and stress reactions (Broderick, 2013).

Mindfulness is all about teaching children how to shut off the outside distractions and be present. In this day and age when all the adults in their lives are modeling not being present (i.e. Fear of Missing Out (FOMO) people on their telephones 24/7), it is important for us to teach this to children. Our students are not born knowing how to be present in the moment and therefore it is our job to teach them.

Here are some Mindfulness resources to help you get started:

- Five minutes to a calmer classroom (http://teachers.theguardian.com/teacher-resources/5879/5-Minutes-to-a-Calmer-Classroom-----Introducing--Meditation)

- Mindfulness relaxation script (http://teachers.theguardian.com/teacher-resources/13303/Mindfulness-Relaxation-Exercise-----Script)

- Mindfulness and the Art of Eating Chocolate (http://teachers.theguardian.com/teacher-resources/13303/Mindfulness-Relaxation-Exercise-----Script)

- Video on Mindful Life(http://www.youtube.com/watch?v=2UF4mmTWsnE)

- Website www.mindfullifeproject.org

- Book- Mindful Teaching- Teaching Mindfulness http://www.amazon.com/Mindful-Teaching-Mindfulness-Teaches-Anything/dp/0861715675/ref=sr_1_2?ie=UTF8&qid=1390190904&sr=8-2&keywords=teaching+mindfulness

Music and Subliminal Messages

Not his →Steve Halpern makes music set at 60 bpm and also incorporates subliminal messages of self-esteem building caliber. It's called "Accelerated Learning" and is available on www.amazon.com. A high school teacher wrote how much this CD helped her high school students and also helped her when she was working on her lesson plans. I was able to purchase a new copy for $8 from an off Amazon brand seller. You might be able to download a copy from iTunes.

As discussed on page 23, music set at 60 bpm is the resting heart rate. When students are upset their heart rates tend to escalate and music therapy research tells us that our hearts will match the music we are listening to. Teachers who play 60 bpm music tend to have calmer classes. The subliminal messages are an added bonus with this particular CD.

The positive messages you put up on your walls and bulletin boards are subliminal messages to the students. One year, the PTO/PTA gave each of the teachers a pin to wear that said, "Children First". I proudly wore it every day. I never said anything about it to the children, I just wore it every day. One day as I was walking around I noticed one of my student's doodle pads had the words "Children First" doodled on it. That weekend when I was up at school, I pulled out all of my children's doodle pads and checked them out and quite a few of them had doodled those words throughout the year. I found that very interested. One student, (bless his heart) had written "children frist".

On the First Day of School

Desks. Seriously think about how students will move through the room when you place your desks.

- Have student names on desks and a piece of brightly colored paper and a fun pencil

- Students will most likely enter with their parents and the parents will want to greet you and talk a bit

    o The students need to have an activity to do while you get everyone in the door and settled

    o Play 60 bpm music as the students enter the room. This is a huge transition for the children and playing music set at their resting heart rate will help them calm down. It will set a calm tone for the year.

    o Ask the students to put their supplies away and to write down what they hope to learn about this year. This will set the tone for having goals, which is something you will be working on with the students this year.

- Be sure to give eye contact and shake the hand of each student who enters and their parents
- Once the parents are gone ask the students to come to the circle area and choose a spot to sit. Call each one up and give them a name tag for the day. While they are putting the name tag on, have them tell everyone about any pets they have or wish they had. This will break the ice for those students who are shy.

Circle Time (for elementary)

The first thing to do in the circle is to go over the expectations of the circle.

Personal Space

Have several small hula-hoops and show the students that personal space is about the size of a hula-hoop. Have two students come up and model sitting inside the two hula-hoops. Then have the rest of the students spread out so that they are a hula-hoop width from each other. Go around and "halo" the students with the hula-hoop and give them positive praise for keeping that space. The visual of a hula-hoop will help them in many areas of the school. Lining up at the door, lining up to get on the bus, the lunch line, and lining up at recess are all places you will want to take the hula-hoop and use to teach line spacing.

Show the students a Koosh ball or similar soft item that can be tossed.

Explain to the students that they must have the Koosh ball in their hand to speak.

Teach them a signal for wanting the ball. You can do sign language for ball or

another symbol you want to use. Tell the students this way everyone will get a

chance to talk. This also helps students to not blurt. You can use another symbol

for "Every Pupil Response" (EPR) answers. For instance, you can have a basket

titled EPR, when the ball is in the EPR basket, all the students can speak at the

same time. These are the types of non-verbal cues you want to impress upon your

students. Visual representation is best because you will say it and see it at the

same time.

Expectations

- Go over the classroom expectations

   o You can either tell the students what the expectations are and

      have them develop what that would look like in various areas of the

      school, or you can get the students to also develop their own

      expectations.

   o "Friends, I'm so please to have you in my _____ grade

      class. I want to make sure this is the best year. In order to do that, we have to have expectations for what our behavior will look like, sound like, and feel like."

o Fill out a matrix on the smart board or white board. The matrix will look like a chart with your 3-5 expectations and tangible examples. Here is one partially filled out. Let the students tell you what should go in each box:

	Circle Area	Desk	Reading Area	Centers	Restroom	Playground	Hallway	Bus
Be Respectful of Others	Sit in Your Spot Criss-Cross Applesauce	Raise your hand and wait to be called	Be encouraging of others	Leave the center cleaned up and tidy	Flush the toilet	Take turns	Walk like mice so as to not disturb the others	Stay a safe distance from each other
Be Kind to Yourself	Pay attention so you don't miss out	Keep your desk neat and tidy	Bring all your supplies so you are ready	Turn in the work you do for credit	Give yourself plenty of time	Enjoy your time outside	Smile, it makes you feel good	Watch for your stop
Be Safe	Keep hands in lap so they don't get stepped on when others walk	Watch fingers when you close the lid	Sit appropriately on your chair	Use supplies safely	Wash your hands with soap	Use the steps one at a time on the slide	Make sure shoes are tied and safely fastened	Use the handrail

- You will want to choose one area a day to go over on this matrix. Take the students to that area and practice how you want them to walk in this area, how you want them to line up, use the facilities, voice level etc. (Don't forget to take your hula-hoop).

- The second day you will video tape the students doing that behavior as you review another area and continue till all areas are video-taped.

- The videos will work for booster shots and for individual review when needed for those who have targeted behavior.

- For ideas on what the videos should look like check out www.pbisvideos.com - You will have to get a Vimeo account; however, Vimeo is free and the website is filled with 100's of great samples. While you could use the videos on the website, it is more meaningful to the students if they make their own video.

Voice Level

Many people tell children to use their "inside voice". This is a relative term. If everyone in your family talks very loud or there is lots of yelling in your house, then you do not have any idea what an "inside voice" sounds like to other people. Here's how to teach voice level and a good activity for the first day of school.

- Give every child a ruler for their desk

- Have them talk in a 12 inch voice- this means anyone away from their ruler would not be able to hear their voice

    o Have them think, pair, share with an assigned partner and practice talking to each other using a 12 inch voice. They will hold up the ruler from their mouth to the other person's ear.

    o Walk around and compliment students on using a 12 inch voice.

- Have them talk in a six inch voice-

    o Pass out popsicle sticks and have them measure them, then use them to practice talking softer to their think, pair, share partner

    o Walk around and compliment students on using a six inch voice

- Have them talk in a zero inch voice-

    o They will laugh about this, but they will know what you mean.

- Use this terminology when you want to control the student's voice level

- You can also make a giant ruler for the whiteboard and put Velcro at 12 inches, six inches and zero inches. Make an arrow and move it when you want to change the voice level of the class.

Areas of the room

Take the students around to the areas in the room and explain how each area is to be used correctly.

- The hokey pokey clinic

- The writing center

- The math center

- The reading center (which can also be in the hokey pokey clinic when not in use)

- The silver box

- The computer area

- Your desk

- Their desks

- Lining up- (take your hula-hoop)

Desks

Pass out books to students. Have a map of what their desk should look like and where everything should go in their desk. Then have the students draw a desk map. Have copies of the map on your desk. Say this, "I know some of you might have trouble seeing the white board from your seat. If you have trouble seeing the board from your seat, feel free to come get one of these." We want the students to draw it themselves for motor memory; however, several students in the room will have difficulty transposing from a vertical plane to a horizontal plane. This is a specific learning disability. Jot down the names of the students who took copies. You will do this several times with things you put on the board and you will soon know who has difficulty, and you'll only have to make that number of copies. Then mention this to the resource teacher in the building for more suggestions to help these students.

Pledge

You will probably have a school announcement in the morning for the Pledge of Allegiance. After the morning announcements are over, it is a good idea to have a class pledge that is filled with self-affirmations. The opposite of Murphy's Law is a good way to start.

"Anything that can go right, will go right. I am smart enough. I am strong enough. I deserve a great education."

You can let the students decide with you what they would like the pledge to be for the class. We want to plant the seed that students are smart and they need to use their intelligence to become smarter. The pledge should always be positive meaning: "Don't, Stop, Quit, and No" are not allowed in the pledge. It should make the students feel like anything is possible.

Ask the students to each make a poster with the new classroom pledge. While they are doing this you can take individual pictures for the first day of school.

Positive Notes

Prior to the first day of school, laminate a piece of construction paper for each student. Three-hole punch this paper for secondary students to keep in their class folder. You will use this for positive messages to them. I call these love notes. The first day of school give them a post-it note to take home and put on their bathroom mirror. At least once a week, you will give them a new one. Here are some things you might write on the post-it note:

- o I am kind.
- o I am smart.
- o I am good-hearted.
- o I love to learn.
- o I am well-rested.
- o I eat healthy for my brain.
- o I will do well today.

Teach the students to put these on their bathroom mirror and to read them to themselves every time they brush their teeth. This will frame the day for them with positive vibes.

Love Notes

Every single day, every single student went home with a love note from me. I sat at night and wrote out individual love notes that said this:

Duct Tape is Not a Behavioral Intervention ©Behavior Doctor Seminars- 2014

Dear _____(I prefilled all the students' names),

I love the way you:

Love,

Ms. Riffel

During the day, I would watch the students and wait for them to do a little something positive and I would write it on their note. I kept these with me all day long and was quickly able to think of something behavior specific for each child. At the end of the day, younger students were called to line up as I read aloud their love note and handed it to them. Older students who might be more embarrassed by public praise were handed their love note and then asked if they'd like to share what it said. By reading them aloud, you will be teaching the students the behaviors that are important in the classroom.

A small cross-body bag, fanny pack, clipboard, or coaster with a binder clip on it will work to keep these with you at all times. I looped with a group of students and was their teacher for Kindergarten, then third grade and fourth grade. These students had collected three years' worth of "love notes". When they graduated, one of the mothers contacted me to let me know how her son was doing. She told me thought I was his favorite teacher of all time because I was the first person to understand his ADHD and his SLD. I felt the cards were stacked in my favor on that because I had been his kindergarten teacher, plus I had had him for 3 years. I had a 3 out of 13 chance of being his favorite teacher. Then she told me he still had every single love note I had ever given him. Here is an 18 year old young man who still keeps the love notes his kindergarten, third, and fourth grade teacher gave him. Do you think the positive notes were worth it? They are to me. You never know what little thing you do means a BIG thing to the students.

Secondary Students and Love Notes

For secondary students, I did five students a day per class. This way, by Friday I had a love note for each student. I did not read the notes out loud. I just laid them on their desk while they were working on an independent project. I put them face down. I did have several students who folded it right away and put it in their pocket. Most turned it over and read it right away. I never found a single one in the trash, so I know it meant something to the students.

Positive Notes

During the day, walk by and leave post-it notes on the student's desks. They will be taught to take these out and stick them to their laminated sheet to take home. The notes can say things like:

- Thank you for paying attention!

- Thank you for picking up your trash!

- That was a great answer in Social Studies!

- Thank you for comforting Pamela when she fell!

- Thank you for helping Sam pick up his books when he dropped them!

Word will spread that these are the types of things you are looking for in good behavior. Kids talk ☺

Final Thoughts on Positive Notes

All these things are easy to do in August when you are fresh and excited about the newness of the year. We know it sounds like a lot to give students notes every day and to leave notes all day long. You will get good at doing these things almost like auto-pilot. Why is it worth taking the time to do? When I would get out my pad to write, the behavior immediately straightened up because the kids never knew if I was writing about them. So how can you keep yourself going?

Duct Tape is Not a Behavioral Intervention ©Behavior Doctor Seminars- 2014

Tear off 10 post-it notes every day and count how many are left at the end of the day until you work your way up to 10 a day. Once you are good at 10 a day, tear off 15 and work till you can do that easily. Once you are good at 15 a day, tear off 20 and work till you can do that easily. Eventually, it will be something you do without thinking. It will become automatic. If the focus of your room is on positive behavior more than it is on negative behavior, the energy of the room will flow to the positive. Energy flows where attention goes. If your class starts getting a little rowdy, check yourself and make sure you are giving the most attention to the positive behaviors. You can improve behavior by 80% just by pointing out what one person is doing positively. If that is true, imagine what the statistics are like if you point out the negative behavior.

That's Not Fair

Some students will need token economies, different teaching strategies, more time on assignments, or a different seating arrangement. Many teachers complain about having to do this because their students say, "That's not fair." Here's how I handled that:

I had all the students come sit in a circle and I called each one up and asked them about a time they went to the doctor. After they told me about their trip to the doctor, I put a purple bandage on their nose. I went through all the kids and once everyone had a purple bandage on their nose. I asked them how they felt about that purple bandage. They didn't like it. I said, "Did any of you need a purple bandage on your nose?" The resounding answer was "NO". I said, "Wouldn't I be a terrible doctor if no matter what you came to see me for, I put a bandage on your nose?" All the kids agreed that I would be a terrible doctor. I told the students that as a teacher it's my job to figure out how each of them learns information. I explained that everyone learns differently. I said, I would be a terrible teacher if taught everyone the exact same way.

Then I said, "This year you will see some students using math blocks or number lines for math. Some students will have two chairs and some students will earn tickets for good behavior. You might see some students writing their spelling words on sandpaper. Whatever you see is what I'm doing to help that student be the best learner they can be. Your job is not to look at that and think 'that's not fair', your job is to look at that and think, 'would that help me better learner?' If you think it will help you be a better learner, then come talk to me and we'll let you try it."

I never had a single student say, "That's not fair." I did have some come up and ask to try different things they saw me doing with different students. I let them try it. Usually, the students found out it was harder for them to do it the other way than the way they were doing it, but I let them try. The students became police officers for good behavior. They would say things like, "Miss Riffel, Miss Riffel, Johnny didn't throw his shoe at the music teacher today, you should give him a ticket." "Miss Riffel, Miss Riffel, Tobey was the first person to line up at recess today, you should give her a ticket." I feel that between this and classroom meetings, the students really looked out for each other and tried to be helpful.

For secondary students, I give the example of needing to give a choking student the Heimlich maneuver. I pretend one student is choking and then I say, "But it wouldn't be fair for me to give this student the Heimlich and not give it to all of you, so let me run around the room and give it to everyone." The kids look at me like I've lost my mind and then I say, well it would be that crazy for me to teach all of you the same way because each one of you learns a different way.

Class Meetings

You might not start these the first week, but then again you might want to start them right away, just to get things off on the right foot. Class meetings are done once a week. I always like to do the meetings on Monday to start the week off on a positive frame of mind. The teacher gets a koosh ball and tells the students about the rules of class meetings. During class meetings, only the person holding the koosh ball can speak. You can practice this by handing the koosh ball off in a circle and having each person say their name. Compliment the students on being quiet unless they are holding the koosh ball.

Traits of Awesome Teachers

- **A**ffable

- **B**elievable

- **L**ogical

- **E**ncouraging

- **I**nfluential

- **S**upple

- **M**irror

Ableism is a term typically used to talk about focusing on a student's strengths when talking about students with disabilities. For many people, they have to see the disability. It is the invisible disabilities that crush a student's self-esteem and potential. In order to overcome the invisible disabilities, we need teachers to be affable, believable, logical, encouraging, influential, supple and mirrors.

Affable means jovial. The ability to see the humor in any situation. When a student comes to class without their books, do not get angry. Smile at them and say, "I tried that when I was in school too. Did not work for me and it will not work for you. What I'm teaching today is too important for you to miss. Here have a book from my extra supply." Smile, smile, smile and be happy that you can outthink the student.

Believable means the students know you mean what you say and say what you mean. You are transparent. You have no hidden agendas. You are consistent.

Logical means you use both sides of your brain to approach anything that happens in class. Students can sometimes send us quickly to brain stem. Breathing and being conscious of our breath can keep the synapses firing in the frontal cortex. This is extremely important in the classroom.

Encouraging means that you never let a student use anything as an excuse. Help the students find their own gifts. Every disability comes with a gift. Every student can learn, we just have to figure out how they learn best.

Influential goes with encouraging. The bumble bee by all rights of physics should not be able to fly. No one told the bee. An awesome teacher can convince a student that they can do anything they set their mind to if they try. Have a positive influence, do not let any student give up. Do not ever give up on a student. Remember my story of zero students failing zero classes. It can happen.

Supple means being flexible. If something different than expected happens, my brain instantly jumps to how I can use that. If someone in my class starts complaining about how Algebra is irrelevant and they are never going to use it, instead of going to brain stem, I change gears. "How many of you like Xbox?" "What if your rich aunt sent you a check for $800? If the game costs $400 and an extra controller costs $40 dollars, how many games could you buy if the games are $60 each?" Let the kids figure the answer:

$800= $400 + $40 + 60x

$800= $440 +$60x

$360= 60x

X= 6 games

That's algebra. Pretty cool huh?

Being the mirror is engaging the mirror neurons. As we mention in this book, when someone yawns there is almost always someone else who yawns. That is because seeing someone yawn engages the mirror neurons. Students reflect what they see and hear. Be the mirror you want to see and that is what you will see.

Duct Tape is Not a Behavioral Intervention ©Behavior Doctor Seminars- 2014

First Writing Assignment

How you begin your teaching of students will set the tone for the entire year. How you grade the first writing assignment is very important. Three Stars and a Wish is a writing and reading strategy developed to raise quality of work and raise achievement scores. John Morris, a headmaster in Haversham, England developed it for his middle level students, but it is highly effective for elementary students too.

Teach the students a second technique first called 3-2-8. In a 3-2-8 paragraph the student writes their first sentence with three ideas in it. The second and third sentences are about the first topic in the first sentence. The fourth and fifth sentences are about the second topic in the first sentence. The sixth and seventh sentences are about the third topic in the first sentence. The final or eighth sentence is the summary and sums up the first sentence. Here is an example:

For my dog TJ's 12th birthday she went to Fleabuck's[1], Boneanza[2], and Barkin' Robbins[3] Ice Cream. At Fleabuck's she had a nice bowl of iced water[1a]. She asked for a sprig of mint in her water and splashed the mint so she had minty fresh breath[1b]. We then trotted over to Boneanza for a nice juicy T-bone steak[2a]. TJ loves to gnaw the bone so she quickly ate the steak

66

and took the bone home in a "doggie" bag[2b]. We then went to Barkin' Robbins for some ice cream as a birthday treat[3a]. TJ chose Backyard Bones Bubble Yum triple dip ice cream in a cup for her birthday dessert[3b]. TJ's eleventh birthday was a real treat at Fleabucks, Boneanza, and Barkin' Robbins.

This technique has been used with high school seniors and has been used with Kindergarten students who dictated their paragraphs to mother volunteers who wrote their stories and then the students drew pictures to illustrate their stories. It can be used with any age.

Three Stars and a Wish

After the students are taught this strategy and turn in their first writing assignment, you will grade the papers using Three Stars and a Wish. Instead of circling everything that is wrong and giving the student a grade, you will write three stars on the paper. These are three things they did well. Draw a line to the item you are pointing out that has been done well. Here are some examples:

- The spacing of your cursive handwriting really made it easy for me to read.

- The use of personification really helped me visualize the setting.

- The description of the forest helped me really see what you were talking about.

Next, you will write one wish. Choose one thing you want the student to work on and rewrite the paper. It's important to set the stage for students understanding they will redo work until it is perfect. You don't want students to feel they can turn in substandard work and get away with it. Here are some examples:

- Way to go! Please add more detail describing the main characters. Can't wait to read it again.

- Nice start! Please work on adding adjectives describing the nouns. Can't wait to re-read this one.

Eventually, the students will turn in the perfect paper and have learned a lot about writing from your 3 Stars and 1 Wish each time. There will be more than 3 Stars and more than 1 Wish on each paper, but the rule is to always stick to those numbers and not put it all in the first basket.

 Here's a fun twist to this thought of by Monika Marcel in Houma, LA. She grades the students' papers using a purple pen and tells the students that the Purple Paper Eater graded their papers. She then takes a smudge of purple glitter eye shadow and smudges the edge of the paper.

68

The kids are so excited to have the Purple Paper Eater grade their papers that they beg to do writing assignments. She said the only downside to this is, you better be ready to grade the papers that night because the kids come in the next morning wanting to know if the Purple Paper Eater graded their papers.

Pencils

Sometimes, students are frustrated with writing. You will know they are frustrated by their sloppy handwriting or their behaviors toward writing. These behaviors might include breaking pencils in half, messy handwriting, or wadding up the paper. Having a coffee can filled with a variety of writing pencils will help. Here are some ideas of different types of pencils:

- www.penagain.com – This company makes a very nice thick Number 2 lead pencil. It is shaped like a rocket and has a nice feeling grip. Students with hyperacusis will like them because they do not make the dragging noise of a typical pencil. Here's a link to the pencils at Wal-Mart -

  http://www.walmart.com/ip/Baumgartens-PenAgain-Twist-N-Write-Pencil/24084994

- Bendable pencils- These pencils are 100% bendable, so the student cannot break the pencil out of frustration. Here's a link to the bendable pencils:

  http://www.amazon.com/13-Bendable-Pencil-Package-36/dp/B00AG47JQI

- Pencil Topper Koosh Balls- Put these koosh ball toppers on top of a cute pencil. Here is a link to some for your class:

  http://www.amazon.com/dp/B00362TP2I/ref=asc_df_B00362TP2I2573647?smid=AYGK33D4ZI MNG&tag=dealtmp477147-20&linkCode=asn&creative=395129&creativeASIN=B00362TP2I

- Pencil grips- Put different pencil grips on a lot of different pencils and have them in your coffee cans. Here is a link to a page with tons of different pencil grips: http://www.thepencilgrip.com/dyn_prodlist.php?k=27468

Test Taking Strategies

To reduce stress:

- Write about your worries (University of Chicago, 2011)
- Chewing gum (activates hippocampus- improves recall by 35%)
- Taking off shoes and wiggling toes
- Get plenty of sleep (Less than 8 hours decreases cortisol by 50%) People who don't get enough sleep score 30% lower on memory tests)
- Eat breakfast- eggs are brain boosting in choline and oatmeal calms by increasing serotonin
- Dark chocolate boosts memory, alertness, and concentration- special chemicals decrease anxiety
- Spritz room with mint- or give mints to suck on- increases alertness
- Acupressure- press spot on wrist (2 thumb widths from base of palm) lowers heart rate
- Drink water- 90% of brain is water- drinking greases the wheel during stress

To combat hopelessness

- Put up positive posters around the school with test taking strategies
- "You can do it attitude" by staff

- Host a family night with game making and review of questions that might be on tests
- Share last year's test scores with students so they know where their strengths are and what to work on
- Host after school clubs to work on weak areas
- Make tests fun by playing games to review
- Teach students the different kinds of questions that will be on the test:
  - Right there questions
  - Think and search
  - You and the author questions
- Dead week- no homework before the test
- Teach tips on answering multiple choice questions
  - Avoid absolutes "every" "always" "never"
  - First choice is almost always right
  - Longest answer
  - Positive choice is more likely to be true than a negative answer
- Work on memory skills- bring in objects on table and then cover and have students write down how many things they remember from the table

To Reduce Anxiety

- Walk around the track
- 60 bpm music
- Relaxation techniques
- How does your engine run (alertprogram.com)
- Kansas Learning Strategies (SIMS)
- Answer easy questions first
- Crank up music before test (Carson, 2011) increases dopamine
- Show 7 minutes of nature pictures (University of Michigan, 2011)
  - Enhances memory by 20%
  - Can download on calming videos on behaviordoctor.org

Combating lack of Ownership (why do I care?)

- Teach students to do self-affirmations (Stuart Smalley)
- Make post-it note affirmations to put on mirror

- Play four corners- to build confidence

- Move desks to where the students want them for the test- as long as it is not near someone else (within sight)
- Let students build offices with file folders
- Cover bulletin boards with blue paper- blue is a calming feng shui color
- Clear up all your clutter- top of desks and tables

Exit Slips

Many teachers do exit slips. In case you are not familiar with the strategy, each student must write down what they learned each day before the student can leave the room. This helps the teacher check for understanding. This idea is a more permanent strategy.

On the first day of school, send home this request to parents:

Dear Parents,

   By next Friday, please send in an empty shoe box. Please take the time to help your child cover the box with contact paper, wrapping paper, or wallpaper. Please cut two slits in the lid of the box (see diagram below). We will be creating a yearlong diary of your child's learning using this box, so it needs to be sturdy.

   The slits should be about ½ inch wide and about two inches in from the sides of the box lid. There should be an inch above and below the slits. Thank you so much for your help in this endeavor.

Sincerely,

Your child's teacher

Then, when all the students return with their boxes you will give each student a roll of adding machine tape and two 8 inch dowel rods (purchased at the lumber yard). The students will put the adding machine tape inside the box on the first dowel like a wheel axis on the right end of the box. (Poke two holes equal distance from the edge of the box). The adding machine tape will then come up through the box lid on the slit on the right side, travel across the top and then go back down through the left slit down into the box. The second dowel rod will be run through holes in the side of the box like a wheel axis on the opposite side. The end of the adding machine tape will be scotch taped to the dowel rod. This allows the tape to be scrolled from left to right.

Each day (elementary) or each hour (secondary) have the students date and write down something they learned that day as an exit slip. This way you will have a permanent review of their learning. This can be used for test reviews, parent and teacher conferences, and to help students realize their own successes. Teachers can review these boxes weekly to ascertain what students need review, corrections, or need extended learning.

Name Tag Learning

Rename your students. If you are learning new material, put all the new facts on name tags and then pass them out to your class. Instead of calling on your students by their own name, call on them by the new facts they are wearing. "Topeka is the capital of Kansas (Sam), can you tell us what the square root of 16 is?" Make sure none of the facts are anything the students could be made fun of later. This is a remix of what some teachers do by wearing a tag on their own clothing for a fact they are helping the students learn.

Gatekeeper

Take sentence strips and write animals on them with a coordinating picture.

- Give each child a card.
- Stand with arms straight out to the sides.
- The children line up and approach -either tell them to pass or tell them to go sit down.
- Only let children with certain characteristics through: (example: only animals with four legs)
- The students have to look at who got through the gatekeeper and determine the classification that allowed entry.

This is a game that could be played with inclusion buddies who pair up one on one with the students. Once students get the idea of animals, the teacher can make up sentence strip cards for any number of concepts:

- Multiples of "X" (any number)

    o Give students random numbers and then allow 4, 16, 8, 24, 12, 40 through to the other side and don't allow the numbers 15, 3, 6, 23,

22, 17, 21, 19, etc. The students will have to look at the numbers that made it through the "gate" and the numbers that did not and determine what the "factor" that allowed the gatekeeper to let them through.

- Capitals of states and regular cities
- Animals that have detachable defensive mechanisms and animals that do not:
  - Porcupines, bees, wasps, scorpions etc.
- Dairy cows vs. beef cows
- Open circuits and closed circuits
- Endangered animals vs. non-endangered animals
- Reptiles vs. amphibians
- Prime numbers vs. non-prime numbers

Grading Papers

This was popular when I was first teaching and I still carried it on after it dwindled in years forward. When I was walking around the room watching students at work, or grading their papers at home, or having students grading their own papers, I never put check marks by the ones the students got wrong. I always put little letter "C" by everything that was correct. If something was wrong I left it blank. The students then had a second opportunity to fix the ones that were wrong. I would use a different color ink to put the following "C" on the papers so the parents could see they corrected their errors. This is how we learn from our mistakes and it also teaches the students that they have to turn in their best work because they are never just "done" with a paper.

Grading Colors

The color red is an angry color and why it was ever chosen in the early years as a color for teachers to use to grade students' papers is beyond my comprehension. Sociologists Richard Dukes and Heather Albanesi (2013) from the University of Colorado told the Journal of Social Science: "The red grading pen can upset students and weaken teacher-student relations and perhaps learning." Thanks to a professor who graded like a bloodhound on the hunt for every breathing atom, I still get the heebie jeebies when I see something written in red ink. I suggest using calming colors like blue or green when grading papers.

Schedule Colors

To get more done in less time, use an orange highlighter on your to-do list. The color orange stimulates the involuntary nervous system. That makes your brain more alert and makes you more efficient. The result is increased productivity and less stress (Tesh, 2013). Try using orange letters on your schedule in your classroom.

Preparation

During the summer months, stop at garage sales in your area. Many of the items you might want for group contingencies can be purchased for a few dollars. If several of you are starting your teaching career together, you might want to meet for breakfast on Saturday morning and then head out to hit the garage sales. There is a shopping list of items at the back of this book. Most of the items on this list can be shared between two or three teachers. You will be looking for things that can be used to make good behavior a fun game.

Group Contingencies: Group Rewards

Group contingencies: Group rewards is about getting the students working together to earn a group prize. There are a few pages of rewards beginning on page 159.

Use things like:

- Mr. Potato Head

  - ○ As you catch the students being good as a whole class, draw one name out of your student pick jar and have that student come up and add a piece to "blank" Mr. Potato Head. Once he is all put together the students get a prize.

- Cootie Bug
    - As you catch the students being good as a whole class, draw one name out of your student pick jar and have that student come up and add a piece to a "blank" cootie bug. Once he/she is all put together the students get a prize.

- Homeworkopoly www.tinyurl.com/homeworkopoly
    - This is a free download that looks like a Monopoly game
    - As you catch the class being good in returning their homework, you move the pieces on the game board and the students earn prizes

- Scratch off tickets
    - Use this as the reward portion of the group contingencies- when they have the Potato Head put together or the marble jar lit up etc., they get to scratch off a prize.
        - Mix two parts airplane model paint with 1 part dishwashing detergent

- Draw bubble letters on a piece of tag board

- Write a prize inside each letter

- Laminate the bubble letters

- Paint over the letters

- Let dry- will take more than one night for it to dry

- Students can scratch off

- Barrel of Monkeys

  - Purchase any color of barrel of monkeys, they are available for less than $10 at toy discount stores

  - Put a self-stick hook on the white board up near the top

    - Put one of the monkeys hanging up on the hook

    - As you catch the students being good, add a monkey

    - When the monkeys reach the silver tray, the whole class wins a prize

- Links on a chain

- o Dollar stores have giant links for babies. They are very colorful and link together

- o Do the same thing as the Barrel of Monkeys, but with links

- o During months that are more difficult for behavior, use smaller links and that way you can catch more kids being good

- Angry Birds

  - o http://pinterest.com/pin/65794844526127798/

  - o http://pinterest.com/pin/108508672241479053/

  - o http://pinterest.com/pin/22236591879621123/

  - o http://pinterest.com/pin/174866398001635953

- Plastic Sink Strainer- Ribbons- Weaving good behavior in the classroom

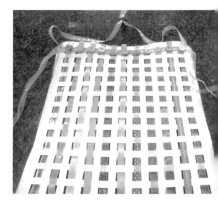

  - o Purchase a plastic sink strainer at a dollar store

  - o Gather left over ribbons and attach them to the top of the sink strainer

  - o As students are caught being good, draw one student's name to come "weave a row for good behavior"

  - o When the whole strainer is woven, the class earns a prize

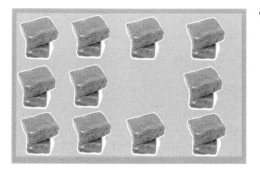

- Brownie Points

  - Aluminum cookie sheet

  - Brownies run off from "pictures on Microsoft Office".

    - Make the appropriate size so that 12 of them will fit on the cookie sheet

  - Laminate the brownies and put a magnet on the back.

- Marble Run- Made from a Pool Noodle

  - Purchase a pool noodle from the dollar store

  - Cut it in half hot dog way (the long way)

  - Attach it to the silver tray under the white board

  - Put each end into a clear Tupperware square and label one "A" and one "B"

  - Get two big shooter marbles and set them on the silver tray

  - You'll choose two students from your name cup and give each a marble.

  - Whichever one lands first is the winning prize.

- Mystery Motivator

  - Like hangman- students flip over letters to find out what the reward they earned

- Marbles in a jar- light it up

Drill hole | Clean up | Put in strand of holiday lights | Fill with Marbles | Press toggle when you drop in last marble

  - Purchase marbles, clear flat rocks, or jelly beans they have at the dollar store and a clear glass mason jar.

  - As you catch the kids being good, you will add marbles

    - I used this type of system:

      - 3 marbles if another teacher complimented my students

      - 5 marbles if the principal complimented my students

      - 2 marbles if I complimented the whole class

82

- 1 marble if I complimented one student- they earned it for the whole class

  - Right before the last marble is about to be entered to the jar, take all the marbles out while the kids are gone. Sneak in a strand of Christmas lights and hide the cord on the back side of a book shelf.

  - Plug the lights into a power strip with a switch turned "OFF"

  - When the last marble goes in, move your foot to the switch and light up the jar. The kids' eyes will pop out of their head and they will want to do it again.

  - My daughter just has two marble jars that look exactly alike- except one has the lights snuck in between the marbles. She replaces it the night before.

- Piggy bank jar of good choices
  - Purchase a small piggy bank and use pennies
  - When the piggy bank is full, the students earn the prize

- CD Tower- used as a spinner with pie shaped prizes

  o Once the students have earned a prize, one student's name is drawn and that student gets to spin the wheel to see what prize the students win

- Pot holder loops

  o Put tons of pot holder loops in your pockets

  o As you catch individual students being good, hand them a pot holder loop to wear as a bracelet

  o Give behavior specific praise as you hand the student a loop

  o At the end of the day walk around the room with a container and collect all the pot holder loops and count them as you pick the loops up.

- Have a set number in mind that you have shared with the students and if they reach that number, they earn the number of pot holder loops they earn the class prize

- Smarty Pants

  - I purchased a Smarty Pant game online at Ebay for several dollars. I use the plastic pants as a holder.

  - When students get caught being good, they get to add their name to the Smarty Pants

- I can draw a name from the pants for any number of prizes including being able to spin the prize wheel, or drop a marble down the marble run

- A real prize the students like is the ability to sit in the teacher's chair

I know some secondary classroom teachers will see the group contingency-group reward and think that it is an elementary intervention. The secondary teachers who have used this have found it a very effective intervention with their students. Let's look at this way: Do you eat at a certain restaurant, stay at a certain hotel, or fly a certain airline because of points you collect? In essence, group contingency- group reward is an incentive to keep students engaged in appropriate behavior, just like earning points to fly a certain airline encourages you to engage in the behavior that corporation wants you to engage in for business.

We have to make it more fun to engage in the correct behavior than it is to engage in the incorrect behavior. Here's a personal example: I went to the doctor one time and she started yelling at me about how much I needed to exercise. I had not gone in to talk to her to complain about my weight or my health, it was just my yearly check-up. She raised her voice so loud the nurse stuck her head in the door to see what was going on in the room. When yelling at me did not get the response she wanted, she started threatening me.

- You are going to die early
  - You'll have high blood pressure
  - You'll have high cholesterol

At first, I was really upset about her behavior as a professional. While it was not an appropriate behavior, it was relevant to what I do for a living. I see teachers getting upset at kids and their behavior. I see them yelling and threatening students with things that are "going to happen" if they don't do the right thing. I thought, her behavior did not change my behavior. As a matter of fact, it made me find a new doctor. What did make me change my behavior was getting a fitbit (www.fitbit.com). Wearing a fitbit measures how many steps I take a day and sends me emails congratulating me. My friends who also have a fitbit see my results and send me emails congratulating me. I get badges and it ranks me against my friends so I can try to beat them.

Duct Tape is Not a Behavioral Intervention ©Behavior Doctor Seminars- 2014

I want you to think about this in your classroom. What would make it more fun for the students to engage in the correct behavior? Secondary students tell me in surveys their favorite prize is a homework free night. One of things I used to give away was free answers to the days' assignments. So in an algebra class, every time they engaged in appropriate behavior for a certain period, they would earn free answers on that particular day's assignment. That way every student would have at least five or six answers correct. It would also help those who students who needed booster shots see how the answers were derived.

Group vs. Group Contingency

Group vs. Group contingency, means you are pitting your class against others. These are things you can share with the "specials" teachers and the cafeteria and custodial staff. Pitting groups against each other for good behavior is good competition and can teach sportsmanship. Students should be taught to cheer for the winning team and then figure out how to become the winning team the next opportunity they have.

I was in a fifth grade class one Friday when they announced the winners of the classes with the best manners in the three "specials" classes for the week. The teacher and I were doing a group project. The librarian came in and announced the class had won the prize for best manners in the library. She handed over the book she had turned in to a clock, which was the trophy. The teacher complimented the class and we began our group activity again. A few minutes later, the PE teacher came in and announced her class had won the prize for best manners in PE and handed over the soccer ball trophy. The teacher was very excited and said, "Friends, this is amazing you won two of the three prizes. I don't think this has ever happened before." I noticed several kids had their fingers crossed. Within minutes, the music teacher appeared with the golden LP and was about to announce the class had won best manners in Music class. The class erupted with cheers.

We asked the students, "What's going on here? You seemed to know what was going to happen." The students told us they had been having meetings out on the playground to figure out how to win all three prizes on the same day. Instead of meeting on the playground to plot terroristic attacks like, "Everyone drop your pencil at 2:17", the kids were meeting to figure out how to have the best behavior. This is the kind of group vs. group contingency sportsmanship we are wanting to build for students.

Here are some more ideas for you:

Cafeteria

Library pockets used to label each table in the cafeteria:

- Cafeteria staff use Popsicle sticks and place in pockets of tables that exhibit excellent behavior.

- Table that earns the most popsicle sticks gets to sit at a special table the next day – or at elementary level- gets to go to recess first the next day.

Tardies to class

- Principal vs. students

- Principal surveys students on favorite songs

- Principal sets up desired percent of tardies 1%-2%

- Plays 4 minutes of student music and 1 minute of principal music (polka music etc.)

- If tardies stay below 2% or (set limit) then music stays 4 minutes of student music and 1 minute of principal music during class changing periods. If tardies go above set limit- it switches 4 minutes of polka music and 1 minute of student music.

Prizes for "BEST" behavior in any special class (Elementary)

- Library- book- golden book- book turned into clock

- Cafeteria- golden spatula- platinum spatula- giant spoon- etc.

- PE- golden tennis shoes- soccer ball on trophy base trophy etc.

- Music- LP spray painted- cymbals- giant treble clef- etc.

- Spanish class- maracas- sombrero- giant paper Mache' taco-

- Computer class- golden mouse

- Art class- giant paint brushes

- Drama class- giant Oscar trophy

- Dance class- golden ballet shoes

More ideas for the whole school

Football field- Baseball Field- Soccer Field-

- Use to motivate students for homework or attendance as they move

  across the field earning touchdowns or homeruns

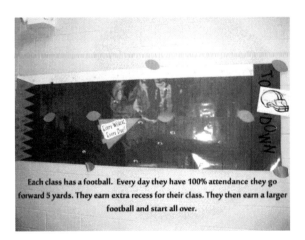

Each class has a football. Every day they have 100% attendance they go forward 5 yards. They earn extra recess for their class. They then earn a larger football and start all over.

Golden Plunger Reward

- Custodian gives to class left the cleanest at the end of the day- the class earns bragging rights- or extra recess- or homework free night.

- The class that earns the plunger has the line leader carry it everywhere the class goes.

- Everyone who passes the plunger must stop and salute the plunger.

Whatever is a problem in your school or class- make it a reward for the appropriate behavior!!!!

Space for ideas you get from your neighbors:

What is a problem in your school?

What could your reward be?

Zero Office Discipline Referrals??? How many of these days do you have a year at your school?

How many would you like to have?

What are you willing to do to get there?

_____

Individual Contingencies: Group Rewards

Secret Agent

Choose a secret agent (hawk, lancer, wildcat, eagle, etc.). Tell the students you have chosen a secret agent for the day or hour and you will be watching them for "xyz" behavior. At the end of the specified time, announce the winner. Let them choose a prize for the class. (See list of free rewards starting on page 159).

If at the end of specified time, the student has not had the appropriate behavior have a back-up student in mind to announce. Then have a private conversation with the target student. Tell them they may be the Secret Agent tomorrow and it would be a shame if they lost the prize because of their behavior. Don't let them know they were the secret agent that day and you gave it to someone else.

Write names on wooden ice cream sticks and put in a cup. Put a toilet paper tube in the middle of the cup. Put all sticks in the middle of the toilet paper tube. As you draw names- move them outside the toilet paper tube. Then you'll know you are being random and everyone is getting a chance.

Very similar to secret agent- only names are drawn from cup for each time you take your class somewhere (specials, recess, lunchroom, and restroom) - each individual student earns the class 30 seconds of a prize determined by the teacher. 30 seconds of extra reading time, 30 seconds of extra recess, 30 seconds of drawing time. Since elementary students tend to have about 10 trips down the hallway in a day that is 5 extra minutes of time earned with good line behavior. (This is time you don't have to spend reprimanding students to be good- so you haven't really lost learning time).

- Teacher's Pick- is a 99 cent program you can download for your I-Phone or I-Pad that does the same thing as the Popsicle sticks. It is all random and you can mark when someone is absent. Here's the link: http://tinyurl.com/teacherspick

Pot Holder Loops

Use as a token economy vestige. Remember token economy is not supposed to pay off with a tangible reward like candy or toys. Token economy should pay off for the function of behavior.

What are they trying to get or get out of?

- Attention-Access- Sensory Input

- Work-Attention-Pain-Sensory Overload

For instance a student with ADHD might be trying to get sensory input- so their tokens might pay off with extra access to a cool sensory input- like getting to sit in the teacher's chair. For older students you can use BoysTown®

www.boystown.org/education. Suit the Token Economy to their likes- but make it interesting and simple. Remember students satiate on the same prize all the time. I like cherry pie, but I would not like it if I had it at every meal.

Student-Teacher Rating Sheet

This is one of our most popular tools downloaded from the website. The teacher and parents choose two behaviors they would like to target for change and one behavior they know the student will most likely do each hour. We like to use a rating scale of 3-2-1. Three means it was a beautiful hour and no behavioral learning opportunities occurred. A "2" means it was a pretty good hour, but it could have been better. A "1" means it could have been a lot better. We use smiley faces with the little children and a great big smiley face is worth "3", medium smiley face is worth "2" and a half-smile or straight face is worth "1". We never use zeroes or sad faces to describe a student's behavior. The child internalizes this as "I'm a zero" or "I'm bad" and then it becomes self-fulfilling prophecy. One copy of this sheet is laminated and the student is given an erasable marker. Each hour the student scores their own behavior on the three behaviors. The teacher scores separate from the student. They get together and everywhere the student and teacher match the student earns that number of points.

The parents are asked to reward their child each night for good behavior at school. So, if a student could earn a perfect score of 54 points, we do not shoot for 100%. The student chooses a prize for 45 points, 35 points, 25 points, and 15 points. The better the number, the better the prize. We have a list of 100 ways parents can reward their children at home for good behavior at school.

Student Name:_____ Date:_____

	Hour One		Hour Two		Hour Three		Hour Four		Hour Five		Hour Six		Hour Seven	
Keep hands and feet to self	T	S	T	S	T	S	T	S	T	S	T	S	T	S
Respect personal space between each other	T	S	T	S	T	S	T	S	T	S	T	S	T	S
Turn work in on time	T	S	T	S	T	S	T	S	T	S	T	S	T	S
Accepts Score (Teacher only)														
Total														

Total Points Earned Today: _____out of 84 possible

Prize Earned: _____

Parent Signature: _____

Prize tomorrow for 67-84= _____

Prize tomorrow for 58-66=_____

Prize tomorrow for 50-57=_____

Prize for 49 or lower=_____

Student Copy of Teacher Student Rating Sheet- This sheet should be laminated so the student can reuse.

	Hour One	Hour Two	Hour Three	Hour Four	Hour Five	Hour Six	Hour Seven
Keep hands and feet to self	My score	My score	My score	My score	My score	My score	My score
Respect personal space between each other	My score	My score	My score	My score	My score	My score	My score
Turn work in on time	My score	My score	My score	My score	My score	My score	My score
Total after we match							

3 = I give myself a 3 if the teacher did not have to remind me about the rule for each behavior I am working on.

2 = I give myself a 2 if the teacher had to remind me a few times about the rule for each behavior I am working on.

1 = I give myself a 1 if I did not remember to follow the rule at all and the teacher had to remind me more than a couple of times.

Be Honest: Remember you earn points based on matching the teacher's score!

Duct Tape is Not a Behavioral Intervention ©Behavior Doctor Seminars- 2014

Young Child copy of Teacher Student Rating Sheet- This sheet should be laminated so the student can reuse.

	Hour One	Hour Two	Hour Three	Hour Four	Hour Five	Hour Six	Hour Seven
Keep hands and feet to self	My score	My score	My score	My score	My score	My score	My score
Respect personal space between each other	My score	My score	My score	My score	My score	My score	My score
Turn work in on time	My score	My score	My score	My score	My score	My score	My score
Teacher writes points on sheet for them							

Duct Tape is Not a Behavioral Intervention ©Behavior Doctor Seminars- 2014

Function	To Get Adult Attention	To Get Peer Attention	To Gain Access to Preferred Items	To Gain Sensory Input	To Escape Tasks or Work	To Escape Peers	To Escape Adults	To Escape Pain (physical or emotional)	To Escape Sensory Overload
Behaviors									
Aggression (Physical)	TUMS CICO	Class Job	Token Economy	Sensory Diet	Equal Choices in Right Ear	Stop, Walk and Talk	CICO	CICO	Assess Sensory Overload
Aggression (Verbal)	TUMS Class Job Private Mtg.	Power Card	Power Card	Sensory Diet	Equal Choices in Right Ear	Stop, Walk and Talk	CICO	CICO	Assess Sensory Overload
Biting	TUMS Video Self-Modeling	Video Self-Modeling	Video Self-Modeling	Chewlery Gum Fridge Tubing	Equal Choices in Right Ear	Social Skills Training	Video Self-Modeling	Video Self-Modeling	Assess Sensory Overload
Blurting	Fidget Tool Diversionary Class Teacher	Class teacher Class helper	Token Economy	Video Self-Modeling on replacement	Vanna White of the schedule	Not typical	Not typical	CICO Video Modeling	Assess Sensory Overload
Cussing	Three B's About Replacement word	Three B's About Replacement word	Not typical	Not typical	Token Economy earning 5 free answers	Could be Bullying Stop, Walk, Talk	Token Economy earning 5 free answers	CICO Power Card	Assess Sensory Overload

		To Get Adult Attention	To Get Peer Attention	To Gain Access to Preferred Items	To Gain Sensory Input	To Escape Tasks or Work	To Escape Peers	To Escape Adults	To Escape Pain (physical or emotional)	To Escape Sensory Overload
Debating		TUMS CICO "Good Try"	Social Skills Training	Token Economy	Not typical	Token Economy	Not Typical	CICO TUMS "Good Try"	CICO	Assess Sensory Overload
Eloping		Teacher helper	Teacher helper	Now/Then or First/Then	Carry a box or briefcase down hall	Token Economy Video Self-Modeling	Stop, Walk, Talk	Token Economy	Video Self-Modeling Power Card	Assess Sensory Overload
Fighting		Power Card	Power Card	Token Economy	Sensory Diet	Token Economy	Stop, Walk, and Talk	Token Economy	CICO Power Card	Assess Sensory Overload
Hitting		Power Card	Power Card	Token Economy	Sensory Diet	Token Economy	Stop, Walk, and Talk	Token Economy	CICO Power Card	Assess Sensory Overload
Intruding		Video Self-Modeling Secret Signal	Hula Hoop	Token Economy	Sensory Diet	Secret Signal	Not typical	Not typical	Student Teacher Rating Sheet	Assess Sensory Overload
Laziness		Token Economy to be class helper	Not Typical	Not Typical	Not Typical	Token Economy earning free answers	Not Typical	Not Typical	CICO Counseling	Assess Sensory Overload

		To Get Adult Attention	To Get Peer Attention	To Gain Access to Preferred Items	To Gain Sensory Input	To Escape Tasks or Work	To Escape Peers	To Escape Adults	To Escape Pain (physical or emotional)	To Escape Sensory Overload
Non-compliance		Token Economy	Assess learning capabilities	Token Economy	Sensory Diet	Token Economy	Social Skills Training	Power Card	Assess physical well being	Assess Sensory Overload
Stealing		Token Economy	Token Economy	Token Economy	Sensory Diet	Token Economy	Not Typical	Not Typical	CICO Counseling	Assess Sensory Overload
Tantrums		TUMS Right Ear Choices	Remove Audience	Token Economy paired with video self-modeling	Sensory Diet	Token Economy paired with video self-modeling	Social Skills Training	Not typical	Counseling	Assess Sensory Overload
Messiness		Organizational Self-help skills	Not Typical	Not Typical	Not Typical	Three Stars and a Wish	Not Typical	Not Typical	CICO Counseling	Assess Sensory Overload

Quick Reference Guide for All the Techniques- In Alphabetical Order

Assess Learning Capabilities

Sometimes students have behavior because they are struggling learners.

Even if a child is in 9th grade it does not mean you can rule out learning disabilities

or dyslexia. Some students are excellent at flying under the radar and "faking" it

102

until they get to the point where they cannot any longer. To consider dyslexia,

check out this website: http://www.dyslexia.com/library/symptoms.htm. There are 37 signs

of dyslexia you can answer about specific children. Make sure your school is

engaging in appropriate response to intervention. If you do not know the oral

reading fluency, comprehension, or computation skills of all your students then the

school is not properly implementing response to intervention (RtI). Consider

referring the student for further testing.

Assess Physical Well-Being

Sometimes children who do not use words to communicate will have

behavioral issues because they do not feel well. An example, I was teaching a

sixteen year old with autism, bi-polar condition, and intellectual disabilities. He bit

himself on the arm to the point that he had a callous on his forearm. He never

broke the skin, but I wanted the biting to stop. After collecting data for quite

some time, we finally discerned there were three antecedent triggers which set

off his behavior: 1) being told no, 2) having to wait for pizza at lunch time when it

was announced over the intercom, and 3) loud, sudden noises in the hallway.

However, some days these same things could happen and he did not bite himself.

We continued to collect data and added anecdotal notes. We found there was a

setting event which paired up with the antecedents. He would bite himself under those three conditions if he had green, crusty, and runny nose. If his nose was clear, those three antecedents could occur and he would not bite himself. We shared the information with his mother. She took the information to the doctor and the doctor said, "It is allergic rhinitis." The doctor put him on medication and he stopped having green, crusty, and runny noses and stopped biting himself. For non-verbal students, it takes some detective work to discern why a behavior is showing up, but it is a marvelous feeling when the team discovers the root cause of a behavior.

Assess Sensory Overload

We have had many students react to sensory in the room when it becomes too much for them to handle. To see what it is like to be overwhelmed by sounds check out Carly's Café : http://www.youtube.com/watch?v=KmDGvquzn2k

To hear what it is like to be overwhelmed by sights, sounds, smells, tastes listen and watch this interview with Carly Fleischmann:

http://www.youtube.com/watch?v=34xoYwLNpvw

To see what it is like to have a sensory processing disorder New-Hope from Autism Parenthood has a short little video: http://www.youtube.com/watch?v=JXWUzmlktws

Go into your classroom and sit down in the spot where the student who has sensory issues is normally seated. Close your eyes and try to shut your mind off from thinking. Listen intently for things that might set the student off. Here are some things to listen for:

- Fans blowing from overhead projector

- Air-conditioning or heater fans blowing

- Construction equipment outside

- Highway noise

- Scooting chairs on linoleum floors

- Balls bouncing in the gymnasium with the sound bouncing around the high ceilings

- Voices echoing off the cafeteria ceiling

Imagine if you heard 10 times louder all of these sounds. You might have behavior as well.

Open your eyes and look at all the visual distractions. Are you overwhelmed by too many colors? Is it chaotic in the room? Do you have things hanging from the ceiling that spin when the air comes on? All of these things can be too much for a student who has sensory needs.

Sit and smell in the room. Is the student capable of smelling a lawn mower stored in the custodian's closet, or the cleaning supplies in the custodian's closet. Can the student smell the food being cooked in the cafeteria? Do you wear perfume? All of these items can affect the behavior of a student with sensory issues.

If the student tugs at their clothing, check for:

- o Tags that can scratch their skin

- o Clothing that is too tight

- o Clothing that is not soft

- o Clothing that is too heavy

- o Seams that dig into skin

Imagine what these things would feel like if you were sunburned. That is what it feels like for some of our children with sensory processing issues. Help the parents find suitable clothing.

Check-in/Check-out (CICO)

Check-in/Check-out (CICO) is a positive behavior support secondary or targeted group intervention for students who do not respond to the universal supports alone. Typically, the school assigns a person to be the CICO person for all the students in the school who need these services and many schools ensure this by allocating FTE to this position. For some students it is very important that this is the same person each day and that the student has a good rapport with this adult. The student checks in with this adult each morning. The adult checks to make sure the student has all their supplies, is happy and ready to go to class with no unresolved issues from the bus, home, or interactions with other students. The CICO adult typically gives the student a high five and some guidance on the day, like "Don't forget to raise your hand if you have a question today." If the student is on a more in-depth program, the CICO person would also give them their student teacher rating sheet and talk to the student about how many points they are going to earn that day.

Leanne Hawken has a number of publications about CICO and how to use it effectively in your school and classroom. This link takes you to her personal publication page: http://faculty.utah.edu/u0026033-LEANNE_HAWKEN/bibliography/index.hml. I highly recommend any books or DVDs she has to offer. I use her DVD: *The Behavior Education Program: A Check-In, Check-Out Intervention for Students at Risk* in my PBIS and OTISS training during the targeted group intervention phase.

It is available on Amazon. It would be a great tool to have in a resource library for a school or district.

At the end of the day, the student comes back to the CICO adult and checks out. This time, the adult helps them add up their points, graph their points (if they are using a point system), checks to see how their day went, problem solve any solutions that might be needed, and makes sure the student has everything in their back pack they need for home that evening. This alleviates so many problems at the secondary level for completed homework etc. If bringing books back and forth are a problem for the student, the CICO adult procures an extra set of books for the student to keep at home.

A word here for the naysayers. Frequently, when I mention an extra set of books for home or someone to check to make sure the student has everything in their backpack, I have some secondary teachers who say, "But that's not teaching them to be responsible." The truth is, every one of us has forgotten something from time to time and those of us with ADHD forget things or misplace things all the time. I feel as educators, it is our job to help students learn to be more responsible by modeling for them things like: checklists, ways to overcome a disability (like having two sets of books), luggage tags on backpacks with a checklist for everything that goes in it. If we just keep harping at kids to remember their things but we don't teach the students ways to be organized, then they will keep doing what they've always done and we'll keep harping. If we take a step back and help them for a while, they will get it and learn ways to be organized. Sometimes, we are not overnight successes- sometimes we have to keep having help until we become experts at it ourselves. Remember Aristotle's quote at the beginning of the book. We want to be proactive, not reactive.

Class Helper or Class Job

For students with ADHD or wandering Waldo syndrome, giving them a class job as the teacher helper is an excellent proactive strategy. I like to assign jobs for all year for each student based on their needs. The students who need to walk around are my teacher helpers. These can be the pencil police (they make sure all pencils in the extra use can are sharpened before class starts), the paper passers (their job is to pass out the papers for each assignment), the etch-a-sketch artists (their job is to clean the white board after each class), the class artists (their job is to illustrate when I read aloud), and so on.

The last job I mentioned, the class artist is an idea that is substantiated by this book "The Mind Map Book: How to Use Radiant Thinking to Maximize Your

Brain's Untapped Potential" (Buzan & Buzan, 1993). One of the things I think that we overlook is teaching students how to take notes. I know as a college professor, it is easy to tell who knows how to take notes and who is writing down every single word that is said. I think in the rush to teach core curriculum, we overlook note taking skills. I believe having a student at the board illustrating what you are reading or speaking about is an excellent way to review what you said and teach students how to take notes in ways that will help them remember the information. Illustrating what you said, does not mean drawing stick figures, rather drawing diagrams, highlights, small pictures, and keywords that will help students when they review. Help the students learn how to take real notes. Doodling while listening increases retention of material by 39%. It is a form of fidgeting.

Dr. Andrew Fuller (2013), in a conference for resource teachers in New Zealand shared his tips for note-taking. He said students learn best if they take notes using this format:

Main Idea or Most Important Idea	Main Notes

Visual Illustration

For those students with low self-esteem, being the teacher's helper can fill in that philanthropy piece that helps them feel better about themselves. One of my teachers at an alternative school I help at is a genius at this. He messes with his computer each morning, just enough that it is messed up and needs to be "fixed" in order for it to work with the whiteboard. When the students come into the classroom, he asks one student that he knows needs a boost to help him get the computer working again. He doesn't make a big production of it, but he whispers to the student, "I think I messed it up again, I know you can fix it for me. Will you do that?" The student fixes it and it has really helped the relationship in the classroom.

Final helper or job in the classroom might be to be the messenger. This is the person who takes the absentee count to the door, the office, etc. This might be the person who takes a book back to the library, or goes next door and asks to borrow an Expo marker. This is an exceptionally good job for those students with ADHD.

Class Teacher

We had a student who came in the Math classroom every day singing, Pink's *"I'm gonna start a fight"* from the song, *"So, What"*. It got all the students riled up and singing along. The teacher had tried threats, detentions, and nothing had worked. We asked her to change her way of thinking. Instead of fighting against the student, use his skill. Tell him if he could refrain from singing Monday-Thursday, he was allowed to take the tune of that song and put different words to it that had to do with Math and sing it for the whole class on Friday. She would give him the floor for ten minutes, but it had to have something to do with Math.

Duct Tape is Not a Behavioral Intervention ©Behavior Doctor Seminars- 2014

The student did refrain all week and came in on Friday and sang a song about using variables in equations. It was cute and all the students loved it. The teacher shared with the student that Friday what they would be working on the next week and he developed another song using another tune to a popular song. It became something everyone (including the teacher) looked forward to on Friday. Remember folks, Adam Sandler, Jay Leno, and Howie Mandel all went to school once upon a time. You might be teaching a future rock star or comedian in your classroom. Help build them up and use their talent to help yourself and your students. See every problem as an opportunity.

Counseling

Counseling can be overused by some students who are seeking attention or escape from class. However, some students really need to have counseling services to help them learn to deal with disappointment, disruptions, errors, and other social skills. Talk to your school counselor and ask them if they think their services would be of help to a specific student. If they do not think they have the skills to help a student, they can help you work with the parents to get the student the type of counseling they need.

I am a huge fan of wrap-around services and helping families get family and individual counseling when they need it. Most counties offer mental health services on a sliding scale and many insurance companies offer a number of free counseling sessions each year for families or individuals. Counselors can help with depression, temper regulation, drug abuse, smoking cessation, grief counseling, and many other topics. It is our job to ensure all students receive the services that will help them be successful in life.

Diversionary

For students with no mental illness, diversionary tactics work well. For instance, when students are horsing around a teacher can refrain from reprimanding them and walk by and ask them a question about their work. "How did you solve this problem?" "What number are you on?" These are examples of diversionary tactics. If a student is daydreaming, the teacher can create a story problem using the student's name in the story problem and this diversion will bring them back from the planet they are visiting to being with you in the classroom. Once the teacher calls the student on their behavior, it is either going to be an embarrassment for the student or a fight or flight moment between the teacher and the student. Becoming a master at diversionary tactics is something each of us should aspire to gain skills.

Equal Choices

The University of Michigan, the US Department of Education and many other research studies have found that equal choices typically result in the student making a proper choice. Threats typically do not work and result in a fight or flight moment between the teacher and the student. An equal choice would sound like this: "You can sit in the red chair or the blue chair." "You can do this math paper or this math paper." A threat sounds like this, "You can do this math or lose your recess." "You can sit down in your seat or march yourself down to the office." These are lines in the sand and they do not work for the students we are focusing on in this section of the book. Yes, the threat of a ticket keeps me from speeding; however, I have plenty of acquaintances who can afford the ticket and are willing to take the chance and so they speed anyway. I'm sure you know people like that as well.

If you know a student is going to give you difficulties during an assignment. Make up a second assignment that has the same problems or questions, but in a different order. As you pass out the papers to the class, whisper in this student's ear, "You may choose to do this paper or this paper" and offer them both choices. Use expected compliance and walk away. Nine times out of ten, the student will choose one of the two choices. If they still dilly dally, you can throw in another

115

choice, "You can use this pencil or this pencil" and offer two different pencils. You can also throw in an "I" statement. "I need you to choose one of these two math papers to complete." Don't ever say to a student, "Can you do one of these two math papers?" The student can say "NO" and then you have nothing because you asked and they answered. You need to say, "I" need you to....

I have had people argue with me on the two different papers and tell me that it is a grading nightmare to have two different papers to grade. It is the same information, just in a different order. I ask them, which would you rather deal with (a) grading a different paper at home sitting with your feet up, or (b) dealing with a student who is fighting you on finishing a math paper? When students have choices that are equal they feel like they have some control over their environment and therefore they choose to take that control and run with it when given the opportunity.

Equal Choices in Right Ear
The right ear is connected to the left side of the brain. The left side of the brain is where language is processed. This makes the child more likely to respond positively to the request, it is more conducive to compliance. This research was carried out in three different countries. I like to add that it should be offered

quietly and therefore not towering over the student. I like the idea of whispering in the right ear, which means you get on the student's level. I like to dip down beside them so that I am the same height as them and whisper on their right side and offer them the two equal choices. Some students, if surprised by a "coming in from the rear attack" might react negatively, so do not do this as a surprise attack. Walk toward the student and smile at them as you are approaching. Circle around and come up beside them, just as you would if you were grading their paper when you are doing your "butterfly teaching". Whisper so that only the student can hear your choices or your comment in their right ear. This way they are not embarrassed and should not react in a negative way.

Butterfly teaching is the time in your lesson when you have taught the group and now the students are engaging in independent practice. As the teacher, you go from desk to desk, like a butterfly and pollinate all the flowers by making sure all the students are on the right track or correcting errors the students might be making as they work.

Fidget Tools
Fidgeting increases retention by 39%. I feel it is very important to provide proper fidget tools for students when they are working. For some students these

should be anchored so they do not become flying objects. This might be Velcro under the desk or a bathtub non-slip applique under the desk. It might be as small as a yarn pompon or a two inch piece of decorative fringe. I like to keep the fidget tools in a toolbox or Caboodle or fishing tackle box. I refer to them as tools and whisper to students when I think they need to get a tool to help them do their work. It is a good idea to have rules posted about how to use the fidget tools.

- Use a tool when you feel like you are having a hard time paying attention

- Keep the tool in your hand when you are not writing

- Figure out which tool helps you the most

- Use a tool when you feel like getting up and walking around

First/Then (Now/Then)

Have you ever rewarded yourself for some hard work? For instance, when I lose weight I buy myself a new piece of clothing. It motivates me to do the thing that is hard if I am going to get to do something fun afterwards. Clean the house, then go to the movies. As adults, we do this for ourselves all the time. For some of our students, we need to put these on a schedule so they can see their work/break schedule. In some parts of the country these are called First/Then and in some parts of the country these are called Now/Then boards. Here is a sample one:

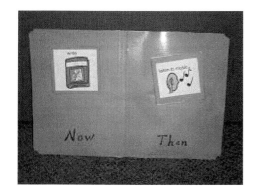

First read, then listen to music. When I am working with students with significant disabilities, I like to have them build up to a 15 minute work and 5 minute break schedule. Eventually, I like to get them to a 30 minute work and 5 minute break schedule. We have to start with a lower amount and gradually chain the work behaviors into longer increments. The pictures are from Boardmaker®™ and are laminated and have Velcro attached to the back. The student removes each square as they complete it and then two new work/break activities are put into the board for them.

For students with milder disabilities, this can be a checklist of events in the order they are to do them, much like a to-do list. When you complete these three items you may have a five minute break working on puzzles or reading your comic book. I used this strategy myself for writing this book. I had to finish a chapter before I could go fix my lunch. We all do these things, we just need to teach our students the very same strategies we use ourselves.

Hula-Hoop

As mentioned in Chapter three, I like to use a hula-hoop to teach students about personal space. The hula-hoops at the dollar store are the best for this, because they are smaller and not like the huge ones the PE teachers have. I like to use them at the beginning of the year to teach students how to line up for the bus, in the hallway, entering the cafeteria and so on. Once I remove the hula-hoops the students can still envision them. For those of you teaching preschool and kindergarten, they are really nice for circle time. Purchasing enough for each student will cost you roughly $25 and once the students understand the personal space hula-hoop, you have some very inexpensive playground toys that get the students actively engaged in proprioceptive movements. You will find a lot of uses for them: hopscotch, base for kickball games, 50's sock hops, or cash in gotchas to see the teacher try to hula and so on.

Good Try

When students say things to try to get you going, you can respond in the way the student is hoping by getting upset, or you can use the phrase, "Good try". Whenever I had students come to my secondary level classes without a pencil, (thinking I would get upset), I would smile at them and say, "Good try. I tried that when I was in school. It didn't work for me and it doesn't work for you. Here, have one of mine." I would then hand them a pencil. I would have a jolly voice and laugh though- good try though. "A" for effort. If you use humor the students will not try to push your buttons. There is a thin line between sarcasm and humor though and it is important to not be sarcastic with the students. Be careful. It works best when you use **TUMS** and have a relationship with all the students.

Organizational Self-Help Skills

As mentioned earlier, some students need help with organization skills. I went over the color coding of folders on pages 31 & 32. This is one great organization tool. Purchasing a luggage tag for each student's backpack is another tool that will help them organize their backpack. On the student's locker or desk, have them make a map of what it should look like if things are stowed properly. Then have a desk fairy or locker fairy leave small gifts for those students who leave their desk or locker neat from time to time. It will motivate all the students to check their maps. Ask parents to come up with an organizational system at home utilizing crates by the exit door and having the students load the crates for the next day at night before they go to bed. Ask them to double check their "A" day "B" day supplies on their luggage tag to ensure they have the right supplies for the right day. (I like to color code the "A" day and "B" day as different color cards and give the students a cue as they leave class to flip to "B" day for the next day.)

For coding homework assignments in their planner, I like to offer two solutions for students: (a) an address label pre-printed with the assignment for that night, or (b) permission to take a photo of the assignment on the board with the camera on their phone. (Why fight technology? Use it to your advantage. No excuses). I do not feel it is necessary to fight students on copying the assignment off the board for these reasons: (a) my goal is not to have students copy work at this point, (b) my understanding of learning disabilities is that some students cannot copy from a vertical plane to a horizontal plane, and (c) my goal is to get the homework assignment home for them to remember, not to get into a power struggle over how they get that information down. Some students spend twenty minutes trying to write down the assignment because of their difficulty transferring from vertical to horizontal. Why tire a student out on something that means nothing when what I really want them to learn is how to conduct an interview of a grandparent so they can write a paragraph on it in class the next day.

Power Card

Power cards are the size of a business card. They utilize an interest of the student to help them remember a frequently used skill. For instance, if a student loves tyrannosaurus rex and is having difficulty remembering to breathe when upset, their power card might look like this:

Blake's Card

Front of card

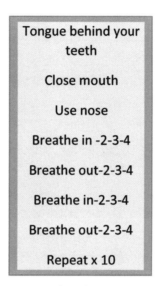

Tongue behind your teeth

Close mouth

Use nose

Breathe in -2-3-4

Breathe out-2-3-4

Breathe in-2-3-4

Breathe out-2-3-4

Repeat x 10

back of card

The student would be prompted to take out their laminated card and use it when they weren't upset just for practice and then they would get rewards for using it when they were upset. Gagnon, E. (2001). Power cards: Using special interests to motivate children and youth with Asperger syndrome and autism. Shawnee Mission, KS: Autism Asperger Publishing

Power cards can also be used to help student learn what words to use. For many older students who frequently erupt, we have written the words:

I feel _____-

When _____-

I need _____.

We role play with the students scenarios where this could be used in the classroom and out of the classroom. For instance, if you are struggling with a math problem and you want to blow up because it seems difficult, you could raise your hand and say to the teacher, "I feel frustrated, because I don't know the answer, I need help." If someone is calling you names in the hallway you could say, "I feel angry when you call me those names, I need you to stop."

Private Meeting

I had a relaxing area set up in the back of my classroom. Students could use this to spread out and work and every day I drew one or two names to bring their lunch and eat lunch with me in the classroom. This gave me a chance to have a private meeting with the students about things I wished to discuss. I always made it light hearted.

This allowed me to discuss behaviors, give tidy tidbits about upcoming lessons in a fun way, or just to get a barometer reading on how things were going in their lives. I always played music for the older kids or read to the younger ones and made it fun. The students still got to go to recess and it was never used as a punishment. Because I did it every day, except the days I had duty, no one saw it as an "ooohhhmmmm, she's keeping Johnny in at lunch" type of thing.

Secret Signal

A secret signal is something between you and the student. Like a coach lets their players know when to steal home or slide into third by using secret signals, this is a way for you to let the student save face and still for you to get your message across. Here are some of mine:

- 2 taps of the chair leg (I was always moving about the room and from time to time to I would stop and lean on someone's chair. Usually, this was because my high heels were starting to hurt.) The students thought nothing of me moving all over the room and stopping by someone's chair because I did it all the time. Each student had been told privately that if I tapped their chair leg twice it meant they were about to have a discussion with me and they needed to stop whatever they were doing to avoid that discussion. No one knew I told the rest of the class this same secret signal.

- I had students who knew if I tugged my earlobe it meant pay attention.

- I had students who knew if they heard, "I spy …….." whatever, I said next was what I needed them to be doing. For instance, if I said, "I spy someone sitting up straight and tall and really paying attention." That meant one student in particular really needed to pay attention. No one else knew that secret code.

- If the student made eye contact with me I could call on them for the answer. If they looked down at their desk and not at me, I couldn't call on them for the answer. This allowed them to avoid being embarrassed by not knowing an answer.

Your job is just to remember all your secret codes.

Sensory Diet
I was at a meeting for a student with autism in a southeastern state and it sounded to me like the student needed a sensory diet. I looked at the Occupational Therapist (OT) and said, "It sounds to me like this student could sure use a sensory diet." The OT said, "I think the student eats okay." I knew I was in trouble

because the OT had not been trained in sensory integration disorder or sensory therapy. Sensory diet has little to do with eating. For some students, being able to jump on a trampoline for 5 minutes will allow them to sit and do work for 30 minutes or more. Each student is unique and needs different types of sensory input. Some students swing, some dig in a ball pit, some need to sit in a bean bag, some need to lay on the floor and have a weighted ball rolled over their body. The occupational therapists in most cases, have been trained and can give you feedback on what specifically they would like for you to do daily or hourly for each student.

Social Skills Training

Social skills training must be taught when the student is not drunk on emotion. This can be done through video modeling, video self-modeling, social stories, PowerPoint relationship narratives, role playing, or counseling. Children with autism spectrum disorders may need social skills training and this is typically who is referenced when speaking of social skills training. I feel it is bigger than that.

In the early 1990's, I was teaching Kindergarten and our motto was "A child's work is play". Our curriculum was academic; however, a huge portion of our curriculum was teaching social skills to students. We taught them how to play together, how to take turns, how to settle disagreements, how to be polite and a myriad of other social etiquette lore. When the children moved to first grade, we were lucky if three students could read, but all the students knew their alphabet, numbers, sounds, and one to one correspondence of numbers to objects and so on. They also had very good manners and social skills.

Now in 2013 and beyond, we have condensed the curriculum and crunched it so far down, that kindergarten teachers are now expected to have all their students reading by the time they leave kindergarten. We now teach in second grade what I was taught in fifth grade and that is not an exaggeration. I feel this push and crunch has done two things: (a) social skills lost out and is no longer taught in school and that is why we are seeing such an increase in behavior issues and (b) it has frustrated kids because I do not believe they are developmentally ready for some of the things they are being taught at the time they are being taught and they give up because it is too difficult for them.

I believe we are going to have to figure out how to teach social skills and the curriculum at the same time and we need to teach it to everyone. This is why I am such a huge believer in teaching school-wide positive behavior support or school-wide tiered interventions of support (MTSS, OTISS, etc.). It is our responsibility.

Children and teenagers are not learning about social etiquette on television, radio, or even walking down the corridors of shopping malls. Everywhere I go, I see and hear people on phones speaking loudly and many times cussing. I see people with no patience and treating each other unkind on the roadways and in the shopping areas and restaurants. Television, even the Disney channel, puts parents down and makes the children sarcastic toward their parents. There are no 30 minute "Leave it Beaver" type shows where children get themselves into a pickle and then have to apologize and figure a way to make restitution for what they did wrong or solve their problems. Kids are rescued now and so their social skills are lacking.

Stop, Walk, & Talk

Much like stop, drop, and roll taught us to avoid getting burned if we caught on fire or the house caught on fire, this simple ditty teaches students what to do if they witness bullying. It was developed by Stiller, Ross, & Horner and is available for download on www.pbis.org. There is an elementary and secondary version of the book and it is a free download. You can also read it in Icelandic, French, and Spanish.

Stop, Walk and Talk teaches students to hold up their hand and signal to the bully to stop being a bully. The student is then taught to take whomever is being bullied with them and walk away and go tell an adult about the situation. The students are taught to be "upstanders" instead of "bystanders". If you will go to www.pbisvideos.com, you will find several videos employing stop, walk and talk at all levels. It is a very effective program.

Three B's (Be quick, Be quiet, Be gone)

I learned about the Three "B"s from Dave Cihak when we taught together at Georgia State. I really like the simple mnemonic because I've seen teachers go on and on right in a student's face. This causes the student to be embarrassed and then they tend to go into fight or flight mode and the teacher has a situation. It really doesn't need any explanation other than to adhere to it when dealing with children who might be going for adult or peer attention.

Three Stars and a Wish

This was described on page 68 as a writing assignment grading technique utilized first by John Morris in Haversham, England. This technique raised his reading and writing scores and he recently won the Queen's Award in England for most improved school at the middle level. John also has the students write a journal each week and write three things they did well and one thing they wish they were better at or wish had gone differently that week. The teachers take this home over the weekend and respond. For instance, if a student writes, "I wish I were a better speller." The teacher helps the student make their own personal dictionary. If the student writes, "I wish Suzy would quit calling me dodo head." The teacher has a private discussion with Suzy about appropriate ways to talk to people. The students get these journals back on Monday with comments and so they begin their week with three accomplishments and one goal for the week.

Token Economy

Many times when I mention token economies, people get up in arms and say, "I'm not paying kids to be good." Token economy was never intended to pay kids to be good. A token economy should match the function of the behavior. If the function of the student's behavior is to get adult attention, then they should earn fun time with an adult. If the function is to earn peer attention, then they should earn peer attention. (Remember the boy who wanted to sing Pink's "*So What*" song?) If the function of a student's behavior is to get sensory input, then they should earn sensory input. Match the function and the behavior will disappear.

TUMS

This is a technique I developed to build relationships with students. Each letter stands for an action the teacher should engage in at the door of his or her classroom. Always stand at the doorway and greet your students when they have been away from the class. The "T" stands for touch them. This means a high five,

131

fist bump, elbow shake, pinkie bump, whatever you want, but touch them in some way. The "U" stands for Use their name in a positive way. "How was PE, Shirly?" "Did your dad get that carburetor put in the car last night, Sam?" The "M" stands for make eye contact. Remember, we have decreased eye contact by 62% since the 1950's. The "S" stands for Smile. We are so busy thinking about the three million things on our "to-do" list that we forget what we are doing with our faces and in many cases, we are frowning. A smile sets the tone for the class. Almost everyone who sees a smile engages mirror neurons and smiles back. Teachers who employ TUMS have reported decreased disruptions in the classroom. It is worth taking the two minutes during class changing time to do this activity.

Vanna White

Vanna White is a trick I employed for students who have trouble with the little transitions that occur all day. We put them in charge of turning over the schedule and announcing to the class what the next activity is and what page to turn to in their books. This gives the student adult attention, peer attention, and sensory input all in one fell swoop and allows the student a chance to get up and actually hear and say the transition activity with positive praise from the teacher. I add that the student should then write the activity on the board with the page number. This increase the likelihood by three that the student will go back to their

132

seat and comply. I suggest using a pocket chart with sentence strips for the visual schedule that the student will turn over when completed. A red clothespin can be moved down to highlight what task is being worked on at the time. This goes along with teacher helper, class job etc.- but it is a specific one for a specific need.

Video Self-Modeling

Video modeling is a video made with model students, typically for school-wide positive behavior support showcasing the appropriate way to carry out the school expectations. Video self-modeling is a video made with one specific student and possibly some actors if working on social skills. This movie shows the student only engaging in appropriate behavior. We never show the student engaged in inappropriate behavior. This is especially true for children with autism spectrum disorder as it only takes a moment for a behavior to be set and seeing themselves engaging in a tantrum etc. might set in their mind as the appropriate response.

I typically take a day's worth of video and cut out all inappropriate behavior and do voice overs labeling all the appropriate behavior. I try to make the movie one minute in length for every year the student I'm working with is in age. A five year old would have a five minute movie and a ten year old might have a ten minute movie. The movies can be broken into different movies for different skills. To see

133

sample videos go to www.youtube.com and type in video self-modeling. The Siskin Institute has some great examples on there and directions for how to complete them. The exact link is in the back of this book.

Planning page for any students you think would benefit from video self-modeling:

Chapter Eight: Odds and Ends

John Hattie did a meta-analysis of the most effective means of student achievement and found that student's measuring their own success had the highest success rate. Visible Learning: A Synthesis of over 800 Meta-Analyses Relating to Achievement (2009) is an excellent book with a lot of research on effective strategies, many of them mentioned in this book. These are some of the ones with an effect size of .50 or higher.

- Feedback
- Student's prior cognitive ability
- Instructional quality
- Instructional quantity
- Direct instruction
- Acceleration
- Home factors
- Remediation/feedback

With this in mind, I made a few forms for students to monitor their own progress for academics and social skills that you can duplicate and use. Each section of Hattie's recommendations have some forms or tools you can use in the following pages:

My grades for each subject: _____

	Average from last week	Monday	Tuesday	Wednesday	Thursday	Friday	New Average
Reading							
Math							
Spelling							
Science							
Social Studies							
English							
Other							

Exit thoughts this week.

My goal this week is to _____

example (raise my hand and wait until I'm called on).

	Make a tally every time you remember to follow your goal:
Monday	
Tuesday	
Wednesday	
Thursday	
Friday	

I feel like I did this well on my goal:

Excellent

Super

Trying and getting better

I need help

For Student's Prior Cognitive Ability

Use Individual K-W-L charts I have few takes on these:

K- What do I know about this subject already?	W- What do I want to learn about this subject?	L- What did I learn after we studied this subject?

K- What do I know about this subject already?	W- What do I want to learn about this subject?	H- How do you want to learn it?	L- What did I learn after we studied this subject?

138

Duct Tape is Not a Behavioral Intervention ©Behavior Doctor Seminars- 2014

K- What do I know about this subject already?	W- What do I want to learn about this subject?	H- How do you want to learn it?	P- How do you want to prove that you learned this information?

Be sure to give the students plenty of options with ideas from Gardner's Multiple Intelligences, the Universal Design for Learning book recommended below or throw in your own fun ideas.

Design and Deliver: Planning and Teaching Using Universal Design for Learning by Loui Lord Nelson (2013)

This is the first user friendly book I've read on universal design.

- Analogy for universal design for learning on page 2

- One hundred action verbs you can use to write observable and measurable goals on page 27

- Sample lessons on differentiating a ninth grade lesson on the Industrial Revolution on page 54

- Engagement, Representation, and Action/Expression are intertwined throughout the book

- The final chapter is from planning to practice and gives practical examples from real classrooms page 96

Instructional Quality and Quantity

I recommend reading the following book. It will fill you with ideas on how the brains of students work and ways to change your teaching to match the student brain. **Teaching with the Brain in Mind: Second Edition by Eric Jensen (2005).**

This is a synopsis of what I love about this book with the page it starts on within the book:

- Top ten new discoveries about the brain page 3

- Brain function- left and right side of brain page 13

- Understanding the teenage brain page 31

- Practical suggestions for teaching vocabulary page 41

- Social skills and the brain page 97

- Motivation and the brain page 107

- Teaching model page 145

Direct Instruction

Lesson Plan Model based on Madeline Hunter's model.

Objective: What is the overall goal of this lesson?	
Anticipatory Set: What will I use to hook the students on this lesson?	
Student Objective: What will I write on the board for the students to understand the objective of this lesson?	
How will I teach the lesson to the students?	

How will I check for understanding?	
How will I give the students guided practice?	
How will I give the students independent practice?	
How will I assess their growth from baseline?	

Acceleration in Learning

Accelerated learning means learning in the mode that best suits your learning style. It is important for teachers to have a grasp of what each student's learning style is and how they learn best. It involves visualizations, mnemonics, tricks, and key points which will make the learning "click" for the student. There are two ways you can divide your class to help direct your own instruction. The first would be to divide the class into three columns for visual learners, auditory learners, and tactile learners. The second will be to divide the students based on

142

Gardner's Multiple Intelligences. Here is a website with a test you can give to your

learners to determine which intelligence they prefer:

http://www.literacyworks.org/mi/assessment/findyourstrengths.html

Multiple Intelligences based on Howard Gardner's Work

Intelligence Level	Students in this category
Interpersonal Learner	
Intra-personal or reflective learner	
Linguistic	
Logical/Mathematical	
Musical	

Naturalistic	
Physical (kinesthetic)	
Visual/Spatial	

Home Factors

One of the most important ingredients in a student's progress is a connection between home and school. This is the reason I use the student/teacher rating sheet and tie it into the parents rewarding the student for good behavior at school. I like the parents giving the same message as the school. I think it is extremely important for the school to focus more on sending out positive messages to parents than negative. I think we should strive for a four to one ratio in our messages to parents as well. I think each school should have a list of each student and columns where the staff write down how they sent home a positive message to the parents. At least one positive message should go home each week with specific information about their child: (sample)

Mrs. Freckle's English	Positives home	Positives home	Positives home	Positives home	Negative home
Johnny Apple	Post card sent 11/6/13	Phone call sent 11/13/13	Text message 2 parent 11/20/13	Post card sent 11/27/13	None
Betty Banana	Phone call made 11/7/13	Email sent 11/14/13	Text message 11/20/13	Post card sent 11/27/13	None
Charlie Cherry	Email sent 11/7/13	Post card sent 11/13/13	Phone call home 11/20/13	Post card sent 11/27/13	Had to call home about fight
Darla Dewberry	Hand written note sent 11/6/13	Phone call made 11/13/13	Email sent 11/20/13	Post card sent 11/27/13	none

Remediation Feedback

Measuring Progress. Each grade level meets weekly to discuss student progress in a room where all students are placed on a wall according to their success. Team works to raise students up the wall.

Strategies are put in place to raise all students based on PLC information.

Restructuring the Day. Weatherford High School restructured their day and built an extra 30 minutes into the middle of the day. Students get an hour for lunch. Thirty minutes are for eating and 30 minutes are for something else depending on the student's grades. If the student is making an A, B, or C, they sign up for an elective class for the week. These classes are taught by paraprofessionals, AP teachers, parent volunteers etc. (For instance, the AP Psychology teacher teaches "Psychological Properties of the Unsub" – The students watch a few minutes of Criminal Minds and then they discuss the mental illness portrayed. Some volunteers teach knitting or crocheting. Some paraprofessionals run the computer lab.)

If a student is making a D or F, they are sent to the class they are failing and they get to work one on one or two on one with the teacher whose class they are failing. The student spends a week with that teacher. If the student is failing two courses, they will spend the first week with one teacher and the second week with the second teacher.

Zero Students Failing Zero Classes

Whatever it Takes: How Professional Learning Communities Respond When Kids Don't Learn by Rebecca DuFour, Richard DuFour, Richard Eaker, & Gayle Karhanek (2004). This book tells the reader how to incorporate this strategy at any level and any size of school. I highly recommend this book as a whole school strategy. If you read this book, you will be so inspired to have zero students failing zero classes.

Worksheets You Can Use

This is the author's express written permission to photocopy any pages beyond this

point to share with others. All pages before this page are copyright protected.

Ten Rules of Behavior:

1. Behavior is learned and serves a specific purpose (Bandura)
2. Behavior is related to the context within which it occurs (Bambara & Knoster)
3. For every year a behavior has been in place, we need to expect one month of consistent and appropriate intervention to see a change (Atchison)
4. We can improve behavior by 80% just by pointing out what one person is doing correctly (Shores, Gunter, Jack)
5. We use positive behavior specific praise about 6.25% of the time (Haydon, et al.)
6. When we want compliance in our students we should whisper in their right ear (Live Science)
7. All behavior has function and falls into two categories: To gain access to or to Escape from (Alberto & Troutman)
8. To Gain Access- see chart below
9. To Escape From- see chart below
10. Your reaction determines whether a behavior will occur again. We have to change our behavior (Alberto & Troutman).

First things first, we should probably define what we mean by function of behavior. The function is the end result that maintains the behavior. It is the reason a behavior occurs in most cases. Function is broken into two main categories:

Functions of Behavior

To Gain	To Escape
Attention:	Work/Tasks/chores
• Peers	People
• Adults	• Adults
Access to preferred items or environmental controls	• Peers (Think bullying)
	Pain
Sensory Integration (Input)	• Emotional
	• Physical
	Sensory (Overload)

149

During Group Time:

Ask Three Before Me.....

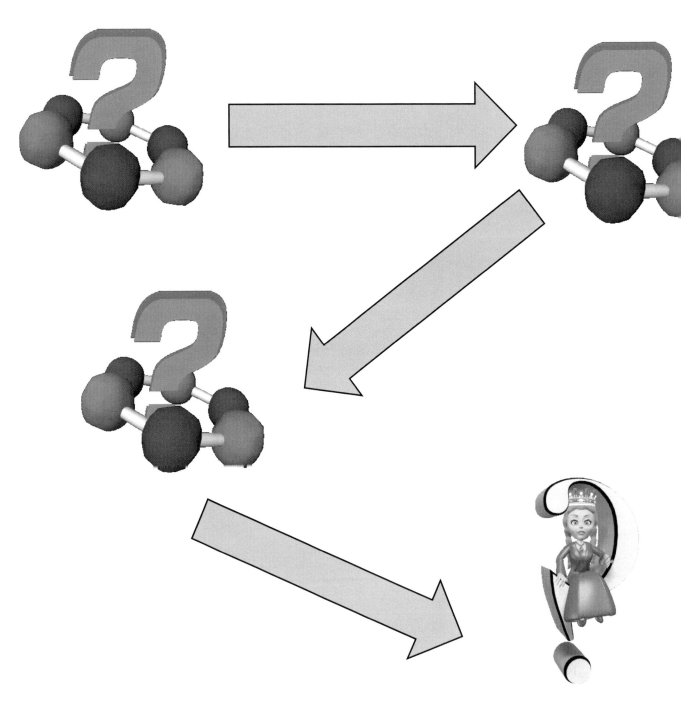

Shopping List

Garage Sales/Ebay:

- ○ _____ 60 bpm music (Classical)
- ○ _____ Airplane model paint
- ○ _____ Age appropriate books
- ○ _____ Any items that match your theme
- ○ _____ Barrel of Monkeys Game
- ○ _____ Battery operated candle
- ○ _____ Battery operated punch lights
- ○ _____ Blue bean bag
- ○ _____ Cootie Bug
- ○ _____ Corn heating bags
- ○ _____ Cushions for chairs
- ○ _____ Cute picture frames
- ○ _____ Desk blotter set (recover)
- ○ _____ Digital camera
- ○ _____ Educational games
- ○ _____ Fidgets (any soft balls)
- ○ _____ File folders in the following colors
  - ○ _____ red
  - ○ _____ orange
  - ○ _____ yellow
  - ○ _____ green
  - ○ _____ blue
  - ○ _____ purple
  - ○ _____ white
- ○
- ○ _____ Glider ottoman
- ○ _____ Glitter
- ○ _____ Good condition backpacks
- ○ _____ Koosh ball
- ○ _____ Koosh ball pencil toppers
- ○ _____ Marbles
- ○ _____ Markers, Crayons, Pencils, Pens
- ○ _____ Mason jar
- ○ _____ Material that matches your theme
- ○ _____ Monopoly game or other board game
- ○ _____ Mr. Potato Head
- ○ _____ Nature pictures
- ○ _____ Large plastic links (baby chains)

- ○ _____ Office chair on rollers
- ○ _____ Old cookie sheet (U can spray paint)
- ○ _____ Old rocker
- ○ _____ Pencil grips
- ○ _____ Physical Therapy Banding
- ○ _____ Pictures of heroes
- ○ _____ Plastic cup for drawing names
- ○ _____ Pool Noodles (you need 6 or 7)
- ○ _____ Popsicle sticks
- ○ _____ Purple grading pen
- ○ _____ Purple eye shadow
- ○ _____ Relaxing nature pictures
- ○ _____ Rulers (enough for whole class)
- ○ _____ Scrapbook
- ○ _____ Self-sticking hooks
- ○ _____ Silver box
- ○ _____ Small round wooden table
- ○ _____ Small statue for student of the day
- ○ _____ Small water fountain (electric)
- ○ _____ Small white round table
- ○ _____ Smarty Pants game
- ○ _____ Stuffed animal that matches theme
- ○ _____ Turn in bins in the following colors:
  - ○ _____ red
  - ○ _____ orange
  - ○ _____ yellow
  - ○ _____ green
  - ○ _____ blue
  - ○ _____ purple
  - ○ _____ white
- ○ _____ Twist and Write Pencils
- ○ _____ Water fountain (table top)
- ○ _____ White metal clock
- ○ _____ Wind chime
- ○ _____ Velcro
- ○ _____ Yellow rug

151

Funk Sway for Your Classroom

Purple bulletin board	Red bulletin board	Pink bulletin board
• Clinic or Spa area • Posters of nature • 60 bpm music • Relaxation posters • Water feature • Blue bean bag	• Battery operated candle • Gotcha tallies • Social information	• Team points • Team divisions if using whole brain teaching
Green bulletin board • Round wooden table • Student pictures	**Yellow rug**	**White bulletin board** • White round table • White metal clock • Extended learning games
Blue bulletin board • Pictures of heroes	**Doorway should be navy** • Pictures of class • Pictures of you outside school Turn so this grid matches your doorway	**Gray bulletin board** • Silver box • Wind chime • Globe

Desk Planning

Purple	Red	Pink
	White board	
Green	Yellow rug- move to teaching area Put desks in "U" shape around yellow rug	White
Blue	Navy (Doorway)	Gray

List of Positive Words for Your Classroom

A1	Bounce	Delicious	Effervescent	Generous	Instinctive
Absolutely	Breakthrough	Delight	Efficient	Genius	Intuitive
Absorbing	Breezy	Delightful	Endless	Gentle	Intellectual
Abundance	Brief	Deluxe	Energy	Genuine	Intelligent
Acclaimed	Bright	Dependable	Enhance	Giggle	Inventive
Accomplished	Brilliant	Desire	Enjoy	Giving	Ideal
Achievement	Brimming	Diamond	Enormous	Glamorous	Immaculate
Admirable	Celebrated	Difference	Ensure	Glitter	Impressive
Aced this one	Certain	Dimple	Enticing	Glowing	Incredible
Acuminous	Champ	Discerning	Essence	Golden	Inspire
Adorable	Champion	Distinctive	Essential	Good	Instant
Adventure	Charming	Distinguished	Exactly	Goodness	Interesting
Affirmative	Cheery	Divine	Excellent	Gorgeous	Invigorating
Affluent	Choice	Dreamy	Exceptional	Graceful	Invincible
Alert	Classic	Drool	Exciting	Grand	Inviting
Alive	Classical	Dynamic	Exclusive	Grandeur	Irresistible
Amazing	Commanding	Earnest	Exhilaration	Grin	Jewel
Angelic	Composed	Easy	Exotic	Growing	Jovial
Appealing	Congratulations	Ecstatic	Expert	Guaranteed	Joy
Approval	Constant	Effective	Exquisite	Handsome	Jubilee
Approve	Cool	Effervescent	Extol	Happy	Juicy
Aptitude	Courageous	Effulgent	Extra	Harmonious	Keen
Attraction	Creative	Effortless	Epigrammatic	Healing	Keenest
Attractive	Cute	Electrifying	Fab	Healthy	Kind
Astounding	Chic	Elegant	Fabled	Hearty	Kissable
Award	Choice	Enchanting	Fabulous	Heavenly	Knockout
Awesome	Clean	Encouraging	Fair	Heinz- 57	Know-How
BAM!!!!	Clear	Endorsed	Fantabulous	kinds of	Knowing
Beaming	Colorful	Energetic	Fantastic	wonderful	Knowledgeable
Beautiful	Compliment	Energized	Favorable	Honest	Laugh
Believe	Confidence	Engaging	Fetching	Honorable	Legendary
Beneficial	Connoisseur	Enthusiastic	Fine	Hypnotic	Light
Beyond	Convictive	Essential	Fitting	Hug	Learned
Bliss	Cool	Esteemed	Flourishing	Imaginative	Lively
Bountiful	Courteous	Ethical	Fortunate	Imagine	Lovely
Boo-licious	Crisp	Excellent	Free	Impressive	Lucid
Bravado	Cuddly	Exciting	Fresh	Independent	Lucky
Bravo	Dashing	Exquisite		Innovate	Luminous
Brilliant	Dazzling			Innovative	
Bubbly	Debonair			Instant	
	Delicate			Instantaneous	

154

Leads	Palate	Safe	Treasure	Whiz	**Room**
Legend	Palatial	Satisfactory	Treat	Whole	**To**
Leisure	Pamper	Secure	Trendy	Whopper	**Add**
Light	Paradise	Seemly	True	Winner	**Your**
Lingering	Paradise	Simple	Trust	Wise	**Own**
Logical	Passionate	Skilled	Ultimate	Wonderful	
Longest	Perfect	Skillful	Ultra	Worthy	
Lovely	Phenomenal	Smile	Unbeatable	Wow!	
Lucky	Pleasurable	Soulful	Unblemished	Yummy	
Luscious	Plentiful	Sparkling	Undeniably	Young	
Luxurious	Pleasant	Special	Undoubtedly	Youthful	
Magic	Poised	Spirited	Unique	Yule	
Magnifies	Polished	Spiritual	Unquestionably	Zap	
Marvelous	Popular	Stirring	Unreal	Zeal	
Masterful	Positive	Stupendous	Unwavering	Zeal	
Meaningful	Powerful	Stunning	Upbeat	Zealous	
Merit	Prepared	Success	Upright	Zest	
Meritorious	Pretty	Successful	Upstanding	Zip	
Miraculous	Principled	Sunny	Unrivalled	Zippity Zoo Da	
Motivating	Productive	Super	Unsurpassed	Zoom	
Moving	Progress	Superb	V.I.P.		
Matchless	Prominent	Supporting	Valuable		
Maximum	Protected	Surprising	Valued		
Memorable	Proud	Tangy	Vanish		
Mighty	Quality	Tasty	Varied		
Miracle	Quantity	Tempting	Versatile		
Modern	Quenching	Terrific	Vibrant		
Mouthwatering	Quick	Thorough	Victorious		
Natural	Quiet	Thrilling	Victory		
Novel	Radiant	Thriving	Vigorous		
Nurturing	Ravishing	Tops	Virtuous		
Nutritious	Ready	Tranquil	Vital		
Open	Reassuring	Transforming	Vivacious		
Optimistic	Refined	Transformative	Warm		
Opulent	Refreshing	Trusting	Wealth		
Outlasts	Rejoice	Truthful	Wealthy		
Outrageous	Reliable	Thoroughbred	Welcome		
Outstanding	Remarkable	Thrilling	Well		
	Resounding	Thriving	Whole		
	Respected	Timeless	Wholesome		
	Restored	Tingle	Willing		
	Reward	Tiny	Wonderful		
	Rewarding	Top	Wondrous		
	Right	Totally	Worthy		
	Robust	Traditional	Wow		
		Transformation	Wee		

I like to take the student's first name or last name and make a positive out of it...

I had a student whose last name was Maze- she used to love it when I wrote
on her
papers.

Positive words from: http://www.winspiration.co.uk/positive.htm and
http://www.enchantedlearning.com/wordlist/positivewords.shtml

155

	Score	Monday	Tuesday	Wednesday	Thursday	Friday
100%	54					
90%	48					
Anything above this line is top prize for the week.						
80%	43					
70%	37					
60%	32					
Anything above this line and below green is second prize for the week. Anything below this line is lowest prize for the week.						
50%	27					
40%	21					
30%	16					
20%	10					
10%	5					

Rewards Teachers Can Give to Students:

Elementary Level

1. Assist the custodian
2. Assist with morning announcements over the PA system
3. Be a helper in another classroom
4. Be featured on a photo recognition board
5. Be recognized during announcements
6. Be the first one in the lunch line
7. Be the leader of a class game
8. Be the line leader or the caboose
9. Be the scout (Person who goes ahead of class to tell the special teacher they are on the way)
10. Be the teacher's helper for the day
11. Borrow the principal's chair for the day
12. Buzz cut a design in an agreeable male's head
13. Choose a book for the teacher to read aloud to the class
14. Choose any class job for the week
15. Choose music for the class to hear
16. Choose the game during physical education
17. Choose which homework problem the teacher will give the answer to for a freebie
18. Cut the principal's tie off and have your picture featured on a bulletin board with the neck part of the tie as the frame. Keep the tip for a souvenir. (These ties are donated by parents)
19. Coupon for free test answer- like phone a friend on Who Wants to be a Millionaire
20. Dance to favorite music in the classroom
21. Design a class/school bulletin board
22. Design and make a bulletin board
23. Do half of an assignment
24. Draw on the chalkboard
25. Draw on a small white board at desk
26. Draw pictures on the chalkboard while the teacher reads to the class (illustrating the story being read)
27. Duct tape the principal to the wall during lunch or an assembly
28. Earn a free pass to a school event or game
29. Earn a gift certificate to the school store or book fair
30. Earn a pass to the zoo, aquarium, or museum
31. Earn a trophy, plaque, ribbon or certificate
32. Earn an item such as a Frisbee, hula hoop, jump rope, paddleball or sidewalk chalk, which promote physical activity
33. Earn extra computer time
34. Earn extra credit
35. Earn free tutoring time from the teacher (spelling secrets, math secrets, writing secrets)
36. Earn play money to be used for privileges
37. Earn points for good behavior to "buy" unique rewards (e.g. Autographed items with special meaning or lunch with the teacher)

157

38. Earn the privilege of emailing a parent at work telling of accomplishments
39. Earn privilege of wearing a hat for the day
40. Earn time with a friend to play Wii Fit (get one donated through www.donorschoose.org)
41. Eat lunch outdoors with the class
42. Eat lunch with a teacher or principal
43. Eat lunch with an invited adult (grandparent, aunt, uncle)
44. Eat with a friend in the classroom (with the teacher)
45. Enjoy a positive visit with the principal
46. Enjoy class outdoors for the whole class
47. Enter a drawing for donated prizes among students who meet certain grade standards
48. Extra music and reading time in class
49. Get "free choice" time at the end of the day
50. Get a free computer lesson from the computer teacher
51. Get to eat lunch with a special teacher
52. Get a "no homework" pass
53. Get a drink from the cold water fountain (There is always one fountain that is better)
54. Get a flash card set printed from a computer
55. Get to dance in class- Have top grade come down and teach lower grade how to do a dance
56. Get a video store or movie theatre coupon (things that have been donated through community involvement)
57. Get extra art time
58. Get to go read in a special place (i.e. a bathtub filled with pillows)
59. Get to play dress up at lunch time and sit at special table (suits and dresses- hats etc.)
60. Getting a yard sign to put in your yard about your "excellent behavior"
61. Go on a walking field trip (earn privilege for whole class)
62. Get picture of self and a friend on scrolling picture frame or hung in the hall on a bulletin board
63. Getting to design school gotchas and have them printed for whole school
64. Go to the library to select a book to read
65. Have a drawing lesson from the art teacher
66. Have a free serving of milk
67. Have a reading party- bring slumber bags, pajamas, flashlight and favorite books- go into gymnasium and get everyone situated – then turn out the lights and let everyone read inside their sleeping bags for an hour or two. Teacher can be set up in a pop-up tent.
68. Have a teacher read a special book to the entire class
69. Have an extra recess
70. Have teacher share a special skill (e.g. Sing)
71. Have the teacher make a positive phone call home
72. Help in a lower level class
73. Keep a stuffed animal at desk
74. Learn how to do something special on the computer- like graphics or adding sound
75. Learn how to draw something that looks hard, but with help is easy
76. Listen to music while working
77. Listen with a headset to a book on audiotape
78. Make deliveries to the office
79. Name put on school marquee outside the school

80. Name put on scrolling marquee with a specific message "Emily Jones says smile and eat your veggies."
81. Operate the remote for a PowerPoint lesson
82. Pick a game at recess that everyone plays including the teacher
83. Play a computer game
84. Play a favorite game or puzzle
85. Play secretary at the board for the teacher (write what the teacher tells student to write)
86. Read a book to the class
87. Read morning announcements
88. Read outdoors
89. Read to a younger class
90. Receive a "mystery pack" (gift-wrapped items such as a notepad, folder, puzzle, sports cards, etc.)
91. Receive a 5-minute chat break at the end of the class or at the end of the day
92. Receive a note of recognition from the teacher or principal
93. Receive a plant, seeds and a pot for growing
94. Receive art supplies, coloring books, glitter, bookmarks, rulers, stencils, stamps, pens, pencils, erasers and other school supplies
95. Receive verbal praise
96. Rent space on a hallway bulletin board to display work
97. Run the smart board for the teacher
98. Secret cupid (leprechaun, bunny, mayflower, Santa, pumpkin, Johnny Appleseed, snowflake)- this person remains anonymous. This person watches all day and then reports to front office who had the best behavior witnessed in the school all day.   That student is announced at the end of the day to come down for a 25 point gotcha. Keep the mystery spy a secret.
99. Select a paper-back book to take home to read from the teacher's personal library
100. Sit at the teacher's desk for the day or a set amount of time

1. Adult volunteers to write a job recommendation for the student
2. All school party on the weekend with different venues for all interests: (students with zero ODR's get to come) Have parents sponsor and chaperone:
    a. Dance area
    b. Basketball area
    c. Game board area
    d. Conversation pit
    e. Graffiti wall (piece of sheetrock painted white with sharpies of various colors)
    f. Karaoke area
    g. Computer animation area
3. Assisting Coach for any sport
4. Assisting PTO to develop ways to reward teachers who go out of their way to help students
5. Call in to radio station and make a request and teacher plays station in the classroom during appropriate time.
6. Chance to go to grade school and teach students about a topic of interest
7. Choosing to do a PowerPoint for the class on a particular subject of interest
8. Choosing what assignment the class does for homework
9. Designing theme for school dance, ice cream social, game night
10. Dress as the school mascot during a game
11. Earn the chance to apprentice on Saturday at a local store or business
12. Earning the chance to be the water/towel person at a sporting event
13. Earning the chance to do stagecraft for any school performance (lights, stage design, props)
14. Earning the chance to scoreboard assist at a game
15. Eating lunch with a preferred adult
16. Free entrance to a dance
17. Free entrance to a football, basketball, etc. game
18. Free library pass to research a topic of interest
19. Get to paint a ceiling tile to go in the hallway
20. Get a golf cart ride from the student parking lot up to the school in the morning and then again at the end of the day
21. Getting a postcard in the mail telling parents what teachers admire most about their child
22. Getting picture on school poster about school expectations
23. Getting to apprentice at one of the business partners with the school (grocery store, bank, etc.) on the weekend.
24. Getting to buzz cut a design in the principal's hair (custodian's hair)
25. Getting to cut the principal's tie off (use loop to frame student's face on a bulletin board of fame)
26. Getting to duct tape the principal to the wall
27. Getting to listen to music during lunch
28. Getting to scoop food at the cafeteria for a lunch period (social opportunity)
29. Getting to shoot a video about the school's expectations to show on CC TV
30. Getting to sit at a special table in the lunchroom with friends
31. Getting to stay after school and shoot hoops with a teacher of choice or a few friends

32. Give students the template for a PowerPoint game (tons available for free online) "Are You Smarter Than a Fifth Grader"; "Who Wants to be a Millionaire"; "Jeopardy" etc. Let them make up a review for a test using the template.
33. Hall pass to leave class 5 minutes early and go by the coldest water fountain
34. Having the computer teacher teach special computer programming skills (kids want to learn gaming skills)
35. Help from an adult of choice on a class they are struggling with (Free tutoring)
36. Homework free night
37. Learning how to do something of interest on the computer (animation, graphics, CAD)
38. Learning how to play chess
39. Learning how to play sports even if they didn't make the team
40. Learning how to run the light board or sound booth for a school performance
41. Let student make a bulletin board in the front hall highlighting an event of choice
42. Make the morning announcements
43. Office aid for a period
44. Opportunity to be part of a brainstorming adult team at the school
45. Opportunity to eat lunch outdoors at a special table
46. Opportunity to eat lunch with a parent or grandparent at a special table
47. Opportunity to introduce the players over the PA during a home game
48. Opportunity to shadow business owner for a day- credit for writing about the experience
49. Opportunity to shadow the principal for an hour or the day
50. Opportunity to take care of lab animals in Science class
51. Opportunity to wear jeans instead of school uniform for a day
52. Principal grills hotdogs for students who have 0 tardies in the month & this student helps
53. Privilege of leaving book in class overnight instead of having to lug to locker
54. Privilege of seeing embarrassing photo of adult that no one else sees (Senior Portrait)
55. Put highlights in a willing teacher's hair (pink, purple)
56. Reserved seating at a school play for student and five friends
57. Secret Wildcat (whatever your mascot is). This person watches all day and then reports to front office who had the best behavior witnessed in the school all day. That student is announced at the end of the day to come down for a 25 point gotcha. Keep the mystery spy a secret.
58. Send home a postcard about positive things the student has done this week
59. Serve as a student ambassador if visitors come to the school
60. Serving as a "page" for a local politician for the day
61. Serving as a door greeter for a parent night at school with a badge of honor to wear
62. Singing karaoke during lunch (approved songs)
63. Sit at score table in basketball game
64. Sit in score box at a football game
65. Sitting in the teacher's chair for the period
66. Special parking preference for a day (get to park in teacher's parking lot)
67. Special recognition at any school event- Guest DJ one song at dance etc.
68. Special seating at lunch table with friends
69. Student gets to pick which problem the teacher will make a freebie answer on homework
70. Student plans spirit week activity for one of the days (hat day, sunglasses etc.)
71. Teacher aid for special needs classroom
72. Teaching special needs student how to play a game

Free or Inexpensive Rewards for Parents

Young Children

1. Assist the parent with a household chore
2. Send an email to a relative telling them what a good job they had done on a project at school. In other words, email Aunt Linda and tell her about the "A" you got on your spelling test.
3. Get to decorate paper placemats for the dining room table for dinner that evening
4. Get to choose what is fixed for dinner that night- example: "You get to choose, I can make tacos or meatloaf. Which do you want me to fix?"
5. Get to help parent fix dinner- shell peas, peel potatoes, make art out of vegetables, make ants on a log etc.
6. Get to be the first person to share 3 stars and a wish at the dinner table (3 good things that happened that day and one thing they wish had gone better.)
7. Get to create a family night activity- roller skating, hiking in the park, picnic dinner on the living room floor or under the dining room table with blankets over the top.
8. Camp out in the backyard with a parent.
9. Get a car ride to or from school instead of the bus
10. Get to have a picture framed for mom or dad's office
11. Get to choose the game the family plays together that night
12. Get to choose the story the family reads out loud together (read the classics)
13. Get to go with a parent to volunteer at a retirement home (the children will get tons of attention)
14. Get to gather old toys and take to a shelter for children who have nothing
15. Get to ask friends to bring dog and cat food to their birthday party instead of toys that will break. Take the food to a shelter the day after as a reward. They will get a ton of attention from the staff.
16. Bury treasures in a sandbox for the child to find. Put letters in plastic Easter eggs and they have to put the letters together that spell treat the child will receive. (Ideas: a walk with grandma, bike riding at the park, etc.)
17. Make special mud pies in the backyard with mom or dad or have a family contest to see who can make the best mud pie.
18. Dig shapes in the sandbox and then decorate with items found around the house. Pour inexpensive plaster of Paris into the shape and wait to dry. When it's pulled out it will be a sandy relief that can be hung on the wall (if you remember to put a paper clip in the plaster of Paris on the top before it dries ☺)
19. Get to go shopping with a parent as an only child. Give them a special task to look for something that you are seeking. For example: "Here's a picture of a blue blouse that I'm trying to find. Help me look for something that looks like this."
20. Take all the kids to grandma and grandpa's except one and let that child stay home with mom and dad and be "only child" for the weekend. The other kids will get spoiled with lots of attention by grandma and grandpa and the "only child" will get lots of attention from mom and dad. (If you don't have grandma and grandpa nearby- trade with another family taking turns to keep each other's children.)

21. Download a fun recipe and let your child help you make that recipe as a surprise for the rest of the family that evening. (Put up signs that say "Secret Cooking in Progress". Must have special pass to enter the kitchen.

22. Surprise your child with a scavenger hunt around the house. If they read, give them written clues hinting as to where the next card is hiding. At the end have them find a note that tells them their big prize. (If your child can't read, you can use pictures.)

23. Make a story on the computer with your child using Microsoft's PowerPoint program. Let your child be the star of the story.

24. Let your child take the digital camera out in the back yard and then come back in and turn those pictures into a story on the computer. Help them print off their book for a distant family member.

25. Go outside and collect cool leaves and flowers. Come inside and put those leaves and flowers between two sheets of wax paper. The parent will iron these two sheets together and create placemats for everyone in the family for the evening.

26. Start a family story at the dinner table and each person in the family has to tell a part of the story. The child being rewarded gets to start and end the story.

27. Let your child earn 5 minutes of either staying up later or sleeping in in the morning. Use that time to read together if they stay up later.

28. Play secretary and let your child dictate a story to you. Type up the story and send it out to some relatives who will call them and tell them how much they liked the story.

29. Write a story for your child where the child or their personal hero is a character in the story.

30. Change the screen saver on your computer to say "My child is the greatest." …or something that would make them feel good about themselves. Do this at your office and then take a picture of it or take your child to your office on the weekend and let them see it.

31. Let your child help you do the laundry and then pay them with a special dessert for dinner. Be sure to say, "Since you helped me save time by helping me fold the laundry, I have time to make this special dessert for dinner."

32. Help your child organize their room giving them a mnemonic to help them remember where things go- for instance teach them the color order of the rainbow and then teach them to hang up their clothes in color groups matching the order of the rainbow (ROYGBIV). Later on when you catch them hanging up their clothes in the correct place draw a "rainbow" award for their good work and put it on their door as a surprise when they come home.

33. Have the bedroom fairy come while they are at school and choose the bedroom that is the neatest. Hang a fairy from the doorway of the room that is the neatest and that person gets to sit in "Dad's chair" to read that night. (Or something that would be appropriate at your house).

34. Mystery grab bag. Take an old pillow case and put slips of paper inside listing some of the prizes on this page and let the child draw out the prize they are going to get for their behavior reward.

35. Let your child dictate where you drive on the way home from a location. In other words, they have to tell you turn left here…turn right here. If they happen to steer you into a Baskin Robbins Ice Cream Parlor, it wouldn't be a horrible thing to stop and have a family treat together.

36. Give your child a special piece of jewelry that belongs to you to keep and wear for the day. (Nothing that costs a lot of money- but something that looks like it is special to you.) The child will feel special all day long.

37. Take your children to the library one at a time and give them special one on one time at the library checking out books or listening to stories.

38. Sign your child up for acting lessons (they have to have earned this privilege). Many universities offer free acting classes on the weekend for children.

39. Take your child to an art gallery and then have them draw a picture of their favorite painting or statue. Possibly stage a mini art gallery tour of the child's work for relatives who are coming to visit. Serve cheese and grape juice.

40. Take your child to the university astronomy lab. (It is usually free). Help them place stars on the ceiling of their room in their favorite constellation. If possible they could paint the stars with "glow in the dark" paint.

41. Take your child on a nature walk and collect rocks. Bring the rocks back home and have a contest painting the rocks to look like animals.

42. Have your child collect some toys they have outgrown. Clean up the toys and take them to a local hospital children's ward and donate the toys to the ward. The child will get lots of attention and feel good.

43. Go to your local appliance store and ask them to save a refrigerator box for you. The next time your child earns a reward, give them the box and help them plan and decorate the box to turn it into anything their imagination desires.

44. Make **Papier-mâché** Halloween masks by taking punch ball balloons and spreading the paper strips over the balloon shape. Make noses, horns, tongues whatever they desire and then paint when dry. You will have a unique and free Halloween costume and you will have given your child tons of attention.

45. Find an old fashioned popcorn popper (not an air popper). Spread an old sheet out on the living room floor, put a little oil in the popper and then have your children sit outside the perimeter of the sheet. Put a few kernels of popcorn in the popper and watch them fly up in the air. The kids will love watching this. For a special treat pour cinnamon sugar on the popcorn after it pops.

46. Find some light balsa wood and create a boat powered by a rubber band and paper clip paddle wheel. Make a unique sail and take the boat to a creek or lake nearby and help your child launch their boat. Be sure to take a butterfly net to retrieve the boat when it goes downstream. (Proactively, you could put an eye hook on the front of the boat and attach some fishing line to it so it can be brought back to shore.

47. Take your child fishing. It's a great place to have some really in depth conversations.

48. Take your child for a ride looking for items that start with each letter of the alphabet. Take the child's picture in front of each item that starts with that letter and then put it together as an ABC Book. For example: "This is Johnny in front of Applebees." "This is Johnny in front of BlockBuster." And so on....

49. Check with your local humane society and see if they allow children under 18 to volunteer to feed and water the animals. (Some shelters only allow adults over 18). Let your child earn the privilege of going to the shelter to feed and water the animals. Perhaps they can walk a small dog or pet a cat.

50. Take your child to the local fire department. As long as they are not busy, they will be glad to show the child around and give them some great attention. Most children have seen a fire truck, but few have actually gone to the fire department to see what it looks like.

51. Play the "Gatekeeper Game" with your child. A description of this game is available on www.behaviordoctor.org (under books- Stork Manual page 60.)

52. Tell your children you have a surprise performance for them. Get a stocking cap and lay on a sturdy table with your head hanging chin up in the air. Cover all of your face with the stocking cap except your chin and mouth. Draw two eyeballs on your chin and then lip sync to a silly

song. It looks really funny, like a little headed person with a big mouth singing. Then let your child put on a performance for you.

53. Play hide and go seek in your house in the dark. Turn out all the lights and have everyone hide. One person is "it" and they have to go around the house and find the people who are hiding. It's really a great way to help your children not be afraid of the dark. You can limit it to one or two rooms if your children are young.

54. Ask your children if they'd rather have a dollar a day for thirty days or a penny a day that doubles each day for 30 days. In other words on day one 1 cent, day two 2 more cents, day three 4 cents and so on. Once they decide then help them figure out which one would have been the better deal. $10,737,418.23 at the end of 30 days with the double the pennies per day.

55. Give your child a nice piece of Manila paper and some wax crayons. Have them color a design on every inch of the paper- could be stripes or wavy lines- whatever they desire. Then have them cover the entire page with black crayon. They color over the entire page. Then give them a paper clip and have them open one end and scratch a cool design into the black crayon. The colors underneath will show through. Do an art gallery tour and have tea and cookies after looking at the different pictures.

56. Teach your child how to throw a football, shoot a basket, kick a field goal, hit a baseball, and putt a golf ball. Then for fun, switch hands and try to do all of those things with the opposite side of the body.

57. Find an old croquet set- probably on Ebay. Set up croquet in your yard and challenge your child to a game of croquet. The winning child gets to choose what the family eats for dinner.

58. Turn your dining room table into a cave by covering it with blankets, quilts and sheets that cover the top and sides down to the floor. Lay inside the cave and draw picture by flashlight to hang on the wall of the cave- just like the caveman drawings. You can safety pin the pictures to the "cave walls".

59. Have a talent night for the family. Have everyone keep it a secret what they are doing and then perform for each other.

60. Teach your child how to darn a sock and then turn it into a magical sock puppet. Put on puppet shows for each other.

61. Take a tension curtain rod and put it in the door frame with some old curtains attached. Let your child put on a talent show for you as they enter through the curtain.

62. Attach cork panels to a wall in the kitchen or put in a large picture frame and put a special piece of art, poetry, or an exceptional paper on the board and have the entire family view and comment at dinner on the highlighted piece.

63. Let your child design thank you cards, birthday cards, or holiday cards and use them to send to friends and relatives. Make sure they sign their work.

64. Buy your child an inexpensive digital camera and have them take pictures and then gather the family with popcorn and watch the video on your television by hooking the camera to the television or upload to the computer and attach the computer to the television. Have everyone choose a favorite photo and talk about it.

65. Have a date night with your child as an only child. Take your child out to dinner and a play or a movie.

1. A gallon of paint is inexpensive. Let the child choose the color and help them paint their room. You can also buy mistake paint (colors that didn't work out for others) and let the child paint a mural on their bedroom wall.
2. Teenagers need extra-curricular activities; however, these activities are expensive. Work out a deal with the karate teacher, horse stable, art teacher, sport coach etc. Offer to provide transportation, house cleaning duties once a month, or precooked meals to get a discount on these classes for your teenager.
3. Teenagers have a difficult time with their emotions. Download yoga lessons from online and do yoga breathing exercises together as a family. Talk to your child about using these techniques when they feel tense at school.
4. Make a deal. If your child maintains the grades you agree upon, does not have any unnecessary absences, and has been agreeable, allow them to take a mental health day and stay home on a day you are home as well. Go window shopping together, fishing, go-kart riding, or whatever would float your child's boat. My mother did this with us when we were children and I still remember these days fondly.
5. Let your teenager play their music during dinner and talk to you about why they like each song that plays.
6. Watch an old black and white classic movie together and talk about how movies have changed. My children loved "Harvey" with Jimmy Stewart when they were teenagers.
7. Write half a story or poem and let your teenager write the other half. Submit the story for publication.
8. Scan your teenager's papers or art work and have them bound in a book (www.lulu.com has inexpensive binding available). Present the book to your teenager at a special dinner.
9. Make a scrap book of your teenager and their friends with ticket stubs and pictures and present at a surprise party.
10. Save your change for a year. Let your teenager choose what to do with that money. One family that I know saved enough to take a family of six to Disneyland.
11. One of the greatest gifts you can give to a teenager is to teach them charity. Sign up to work in a soup kitchen, nursing home, or other similar area and work with them once a month.
12. Organize a neighborhood football or basketball game "oldies" vs. "youngsters" or "men" vs. "women" and then have a block barbecue afterwards.
13. Let them drive the "good" car for a special occasion.
14. Surprise them with their favorite dessert for no special reason.
15. Write a story about the 20 things you love about them. Include fun pictures.
16. Choose a family member of the month and make a poster of them. Let them choose Friday night dinners for the month.
17. Teach your children how to play a game like *Spoons, Canasta, Poker*, etc. and have a family game night.
18. Turn out all the lights in the house and play hide and go seek in the dark. The person that can stay hidden the longest gets to choose the movie the family watches on Saturday night.
19. Hire your child to be an interior decorator and using only items available in the house, redo a room in the house.

20. Do your own *Trading Spaces*. Parents redecorate the teen's bedroom and the teen redecorates the parent's bedroom.
21. Use plastic Easter eggs and put dollar amounts in the eggs on slips of paper and number the eggs with a permanent marker. Play *Deal or No Deal* with one of the parents playing the banker.
22. Help your teenager study for a test by downloading a free *Who Wants to be a Millionaire* PowerPoint game and put the answers to your teenagers' test into the game and then play to help them study.
23. Tape record your student's study questions onto a tape recorder for them so they can listen to them while they are going to sleep.
24. Make flash cards for your student's exams to help them study for a big exam.
25. Help your teenager organize their notebook using color coded folders for each subject and pocket folders for study cards.
26. Hide positive messages all over your teenager's room, in their books they use at home (you don't want them to get embarrassed at school), on their bathroom mirror, etc.
27. Watch Jeopardy and give each family member a pad of post it notes or index cards. Have everyone write down what they think the answer is and keep points. The person who wins gets to pick what the family does as an activity that weekend.
28. Do some research for your teenager. For example, if your teen is studying Greek Mythology go to the library and check out all the books on Greek Mythology for them or download some appropriate materials from the Internet (be careful of the Internet as some information is not correct).
29. Take your teen to a museum, on a nature walk, to a sporting event, whatever would float their boat. It's the time you spend with them that is important and there are many free events you can attend.
30. Make a special mix CD for your teen of their favorite songs. You can upload i-tunes and then copy their own CD's into the program and mix and match their favorite songs onto one CD so they don't have to flip through CD's to listen to their favorite songs.
31. Have a contest to see who can find something that no one in the family can guess what it is. For example, a shirt stay, or the inside spring to a toy, things that might not be recognizable away from their use.
32. Have everyone come to the table with a quote and then a contest to see who can guess who made the quote famous.
33. Surprise your teen with a scavenger hunt all over the house when they get home from school. Make the clues hard to figure out. I always had a little prize at the end like baseball cards.
34. Let your teen host the training of a guide dog. This will teach them responsibility and give them a sense of pride.
35. Help your teen become a big brother or sister to a child who needs a mentor. There is no greater gift you can give yourself than that of service to someone in need.

For 32 pages of Free Rewards for Educators follow this link:

http://behaviordoctor.org/files/tools/2013rewardsforfree.docx

Tweets

Some of my favorite links – from www.twitter.com/behaviordoctor - Be sure to follow:

ADHD Parenting Tips- http://voices.yahoo.com/parenting-child-adhd-5-parenting-years-7206666.html?cat=25

Classroom Modifications for the student with Autism-

http://www.bellaonline.com/articles/art35123.asp

Exercise for Oppositional Defiant Disorder-

http://www.livestrong.com/article/442252-exercises-for-oppositional-defiant-disorder/

Fidgeting-http://www.ncbi.nlm.nih.gov/pmc/articles/PMC3776418/ (2013)

Five Brain Exercise Activities for Children with ADHD -

http://www.empoweringparents.com/Five-Simple-Brain-Exercise-Activities-for-Your-ADHD-Child.php

Helping Children with ADHD Succeed in School-

http://www.helpguide.org/mental/adhd_add_teaching_strategies.htm

How Mental Focus and Exercise Can Beat Bi-Polar Disorder-

http://www.livinghealthy360.com/index.php/how-mental-focus-and-exercise-can-beat-bipolar-disorder-42824/

Managing meltdowns for students with Asperger's-

http://suite101.com/a/managing-meltdowns-in-children-with-aspergers-a392398

Oppositional Defiant Disorder- Improve Sleep with Classical Music-

http://voices.yahoo.com/oppositional-defiance-disorder-improve-sleep-with-3970376.html?cat=70

Parenting Your ADHD Teen About Making Good Decisions on Alcohol and Drugs-

http://add.about.com/od/childrenandteens/a/haffner.htm

Reading Comprehension and ADHD-

http://link.springer.com/article/10.1007%2Fs10802-012-9686-8#page-1

Reducing Anxiety-

http://www.reddit.com/r/science/comments/1fptiu/scientists_have_found_that_meditation_can_reduce/

Scientists say "Taking Away Recess is Bad for Kids with ADHD" -

http://www.livescience.com/20557-adhd-exercise-recess-improve-behavior.html

Sensory Diet Tips-

http://communicationstationspeechtx.blogspot.com/2013/04/tip-tuesday-autism-and-sensory-diet.html

Ten Facts You May Not Know About ADHD-

http://link.springer.com/article/10.1007%2Fs10802-012-9686-8#page-1

Ten Myths About ADHD- http://www.parents.com/toddlers-preschoolers/health/add/10-addadhd-myths/

The Effect of Bi-Polar Disorder on the Developmental Process -

http://www.dhinfo.org/2011/03/the-effect-of-bipolar-disorder-on-a-child%E2%80%99s-development-process/

Three Reasons Why Children with Autism Tend to Wander-

http://health.clevelandclinic.org/2013/02/children-with-autism-tend-wander/

TICS and ADHD- http://add.about.com/od/childrenandteens/a/tics-adhd.htm

Tips for teaching students with Autism-

http://www.pathfindersforautism.org/articles/view/educational-recommendations-for-autism-spectrum-disorders

References

Berman, M.; Jonides, J.; & Kaplan, S. (2008). The cognitive benefits of interacting with nature. *Psychological Science, 19.* (12). (University of Michigan Study)

Broderick, P. (2013). *Learning to breathe: A mindfulness curriculum for adolescents to cultivate emotion regulation, attention, and performance.* Oakland, CA: New Harbinger.

Buzan, T. & Buzan, B. (1993). *Learning to breathe: A mindfulness curriculum for adolescents to cultivate emotion regulation, attention, and performance.* New York, NY: Penguin.

Carson, S. (2010). *Your creative brain: Seven steps to maximize imagination, productivity, and innovation in your life.* Boston, MA: Harvard Health Press.

Dukes, R. & Albanesi, H. (2012) Seeing red: Quality of an essay, color of the grading pen, and student reactions to the grading process. *The Social Science Journal,49.*

DuFour, R., Eaker, R., Karhanek, G., & DuFour, R. (2004). *Whatever it takes: How professional learning communities respond when kids don't learn.* Bloomington, IN: Solution Tree.

Farley, J.; Risko, E.; & Kingstone, A. (2013). Everyday attention and lecture retention: The effects of time, fidgeting, and mind wandering. *Frontiers in Psychology (4),* 619. (Also reported in National Institute of Health)

Fuller, A. (2013). Tricky kids: Transforming conflict and freeing their potential. New York, NY: Harper Collins.

Gagnon, E. (2001). *Power cards: Using special interests to motivate children and youth with Asperger syndrome and autism.* Shawnee Mission, KS: Autism Asperger Publishing.

Harms, W. (2011). Writing about your worries eases anxiety and improves test performance. University of Chicago. Retrieved February 1, 2014. http://news.uchicago.edu/article/2011/01/13/writing-about-worries-eases-anxiety-and-improves-test-performance

Hattie, J. (2008). *Visible Learning: A synthesis of over 800 meta-analyses relating to achievement.* New York, NY: Routledge

Heiss, E. (2004). *Feng Shui for the classroom: 101 easy to use ideas.* Chicago, IL: Zephyr Press.

Jensen, E. (2005). *Teaching with the Brain in Mind.* Alexandria, VA. ASCD

Küller R, Laike T. (1998). The impact of flicker from fluorescent lighting on well-being, performance and physiological arousal. *Ergonomics 41* (4): 433-47.

National Education Association (NEA). (2013) Feng Shui: retrieved on February 1, 2014 http://www.nea.org/tools/feng-shui-for-the-classroom.html

Nelson, L. (2013). *Design and Deliver.* Baltimore, MD: Brookes Publishing.

Schoeberlen, D. (2009). *Mindful teaching and teaching mindfulness: A guide for anyone who teaches anything.* Boston, MA: Wisdom Publications.

Tesh, J. (2013). Highlighting in orange causes cognitive awareness. Intelligence for your life. Radio broadcast.

Websites

Reducing anxiety by 39%: http://www.psychcongress.com/article/mri-shows-how-meditation-alleviates-anxiety-11894

Reducing stress: http://annerivendell.hubpages.com/hub/6-Top-Tips-for-relaxation-and-stress-reduction

Stress Relief: http://www.stress-relief-tools.com/muscle-relaxation-technique.html

Strategic Intervention Model (Kansas Learning Strategies) http://www.ku-crl.org/sim/

Fitbit- www.fitbit.com

Nature Break Reduces Stress: http://dirt.asla.org/2011/09/08/research-shows-nature-helps-with-stress/

Movie Clips Used in the Presentation

Born to Create Drama: http://www.youtube.com/watch?v=Pzl86IjTpHI

Dr. Emoto: Power of Words: http://www.youtube.com/watch?v=iu9P167HLsw

Power of Words: (blind man): http://www.youtube.com/watch?v=OqOzxZss5WA

Power of Touch: http://www.youtube.com/watch?v=bx2wFhjb9Oo

Power of Using Names: http://www.youtube.com/watch?v=6XLU3FeQJNA

(funny)

Power of Eye Contact: http://www.youtube.com/watch?v=4LLTq6Ex4Z8

Power of a Smile: http://www.youtube.com/watch?v=U9cGdRNMdQQ

Video Self-Modeling: http://www.youtube.com/watch?v=m0yj-TKbvnI

This is a test. Please read everything first and be ready to hand in at the end of this session:

1. Put your name in the top left hand corner of this paper.

2. Circle all the odd numbers on this paper.

3. In the lower left hand corner write down what street you lived on when you were 5 years old.

4. Turn to the person on your right and ask them where they were born and write it here:

   _____.

5. Which would you rather have: a) one dollar a day for a month or b) one penny on day one and then doubled on day two, that doubled on day three and so on for 30 days?

6. What do you think Dr. Riffel's middle name is?

7. How old do you think Dr. Riffel is?

8. What is your favorite color? _____

9. What is your favorite number? _____

10. What is the answer to this? X + 5X= 30 _____

11. What is the longest river in the world? _____

12. By the way, in question number 5- you would have 30 dollars if you took the dollar or you would have $5,368,709.12 by the end of 30 days. Now which one do you want?

13. How many miles is it to the sun? _____

14. How many times does the earth rotate around the sun in one year? _____

15. Name an animal that is yellow: _____

16. What was your first pet? _____

17. Turn to your neighbor on the left and ask them what their favorite color is: _____

18. What is the answer to this problem: What is 365 x 24 x 60? _____

19. Only answer the first question: _____